Exploring God's Promises

PEACE

Exploring God's Promises

PEACE

Inspiring True Stories
of
God's Promise Fulfilled

EDITORS OF GUIDEPOSTS

Exploring God's Promises: Peace

Published by Guideposts
100 Reserve Road, Suite E200
Danbury, CT 06810
Guideposts.org

Acknowledgments

Every attempt has been made to credit the sources of copyrighted material used in this book. If any such acknowledgment has been inadvertently omitted or miscredited, receipt of such information would be appreciated.

Cover design by Serena Fox, Bean Inc.
Interior design by Serena Fox, Bean Inc.
Cover photo © Shutterstock 1856837941 Natspace
Typeset by Aptara, Inc.

ISBN 978-1-961125-83-4 (hardcover)
ISBN 978-1-965859-79-7 (softcover
ISBN 978-1-961125-84-1 (epub)

Printed and bound in the United States of America

Never be in a hurry; do everything quietly and in a calm spirit. Do not lose your inner peace for anything whatsoever, even if your whole world seems upset.

—Saint Francis de Sales

CONTENTS

PREFACE

A DEEP AND UNWAVERING PEACE

By Claire McGarry

WE ALL YEARN for peace and look for it in different places. After searching for it over the years, I'd like to propose that true peace is found in love.

If you've ever fallen head over heels in love with another person, you know what I mean. Nothing phases you during that honeymoon period. I experienced it firsthand with my husband, John. There were times when I ran out of gas on the highway, lost my purse with cash and credit cards inside, and fell and twisted my ankle. None of those things undid me. None of them stole my serenity. I considered those events and other problems just minor bumps in the road because I was in love with John and viewing life through rose-colored glasses. Having him by my side was enough to calm my soul. Moreover, John was at the ready to rescue me in every one of those situations. Through it all, he loved me exactly as I am, without judgment, without keeping score.

Sadly, honeymoon periods do end. John and I still love and support each other, but we have a flawed and earthly relationship. We both make mistakes. We're prone to bicker, compete, and reopen old wounds.

The relationship God offers us, however, can be divine if we embrace the heavenly aspect of it. As the Source of love itself, He is unconditional and unchanging. His love comes with no strings attached, no trace of judgment, and no need to earn it or deserve it. He doles it out graciously and lavishly. We just need to turn to Him to receive it.

And when we do? Peace abounds! The deeper we entwine our heart in His, grounding our days in His Word and in His presence, the more peaceful they will be. Sure, we may still lose our car keys, miss a deadline for work, or get bad news from the doctor. However, when we view these problems through God-colored glasses, we're able to look past them and focus on Him to calm our soul. We can feel tranquil—peaceful—despite the pitfalls or mountains in our path because we know His love for us is constant and pure.

Moreover, just as John was there to rescue me, God is always ready and waiting to rescue us at every turn. Isaiah 46:4 (NIV) says: "Even to your old age and gray hairs I am he, I am he who will sustain you. I have made you and I will carry you; I will sustain you and I will rescue you."

Unfortunately, many people misinterpret what God means when He vows to rescue us, defaulting to society's definition of "rescue," thinking it results in an easy life, one without conflict or hardship. Worse yet, we let social media and its images of the perfect family, beautiful home, and exotic vacations bombard us constantly, further convincing us that a life other than the one God has given us is what will fill us with abundant joy.

Peace Is an Inside Job

The truth is the complete opposite. John 14:27 (NIV) says: "Peace I leave with you; my peace I give you. I do not give to you as the world gives." True peace isn't about how things look on the outside. If we only feel calm when things are good, we're fastening our heart to our circumstances, giving serenity permission to come and go based on the ups and downs of life. That's not peace at all. It's actually pleasure, and pleasure is a fleeting emotion.

I experienced the difference on our recent family vacation. We had saved for the trip for over a year and spent the weeks leading up to it planning fun activities and excursions. Unfortunately, less than twenty-four hours after we left home, I sustained an injury that almost ruined it all. As we were exploring the shores of Lake George, New York, I slipped and fell on a wet dock. Up I went like a cartoon character with both legs flying into the air. When I came crashing down, I landed my full body weight on my left elbow. I've experienced a lot of pain in my life, but that fall had me gasping for air and reeling in agony. I didn't break any bones, but my elbow was so bruised that I couldn't bend it or use my entire left arm for days, to the point where my daughter had to dress and undress me.

The next day, as my husband and kids went kayaking, I had no choice but to stay back and nurse my wounds—both the pain in my arm and the ache in my heart. I could already tell I wasn't going to be able to participate in most of the remaining activities; I'd be a bystander on my own vacation. In my dejection, I turned to God in prayer, reflecting on what I was reading in that day's devotional, a passage from Matthew 13. I was so uncomfortable, I couldn't concentrate beyond verse 16 (NIV): "But blessed are your eyes because they see, and your ears because they hear."

My mind began to wander, and that verse kept repeating in my head. Without any conscious thought at all, it morphed into "Blessed am I." The more that new mantra repeated in my mind, the more my heart aligned with the words. Yes—my injury was preventing me from physically participating in the fun. But it was my self-pity that was preventing me from participating with my heart. I could still be with my family during meals and downtime, playing games and making memories in other ways. I was on vacation after all—away from the demands of life, with the people that mean the most in the world to me. Blessed was I, indeed!

From that point on, I enjoyed every minute of that vacation—not because God outwardly healed me and took away the pain in my arm, but because He rescued me inwardly, taking away the pain in my heart and replacing it with peace and gratitude, even as my elbow continued to throb.

That experience gave the verse in Matthew 13:16 a whole new meaning. When I was using my eyes to see only the negative and my ears to hear only the complaints in my heart, I was blind and deaf to the gifts before me. It took God's grace to heal my perspective, opening the eyes and ears of my heart so I could experience the peace He was offering me in the midst of my pain and disappointment.

Shifting Our Perspective to Recognize Peace

In 1915, Danish psychologist Edgar Rubin created the black-and-white image called Rubin's vase. When you focus on the white space, you see a vase. When you focus on the black space, you see two faces. It's an example of how things change depending on viewpoint, perspective, or context.

God gave us free will, and with that comes the freedom to choose how we view things. Are we going to focus on the dark struggles in our lives that have the power to eclipse our days and steal our peace? Or are we going to focus on the bright spaces where God's light is shining through, casting out shadows and exuding grace? When we look to the Light of the World with complete trust, we submit to His will for us, sure in the fact that He's always working for our good (Romans 8:28).

Of course, it's easy to see the good in a true and complete healing. But can we see the good when a burden isn't removed? Difficult situations tell us the truth about who we really are and how authentic our faith is. Does our belief evaporate like steam when the heat is turned up? Do we cling to the false peace of this world that slips through our fingers any time something doesn't go our way?

I learned that difficulties can become second chances to practice trust. If we use them like a forger's fire to burn away whatever negative emotions are entwined around our heart, they refine us—and perfect our faith. Just as lifting heavy things strengthens our physical muscles, bearing up under our struggles with grace strengthens our spiritual muscles. God is with us through it all, strengthening and helping us (Isaiah 41:10) to grow stronger in heart and mind. Consequently, our inner serenity becomes so resolute that the outer waves of adversity can't wash it away.

This doesn't happen, though, without consciously turning to God over and over again. In the same way our earthly relationships are nurtured by time spent together, our Heavenly relationship needs our attention too—not for God, but for us.

Peace Flourishes in Relationships

When my oldest son, Zack, went off to college last year, I longed for him to call or text. I wanted to hear about every aspect of his experience. I was curious about the new people he was meeting, the classes he was taking, the clubs he was joining, and how he was adjusting to being away from home. I'd gone to college myself, way back when, and had experienced the ups and downs of being on my own for the first time. I felt I had the wisdom and experience to help him through it. But no one wants unsolicited advice, especially a teenage boy. I couldn't be a helicopter parent, forcing my guidance down his throat. It was up to him to ask me for it. It was also up to him to decide what he was and wasn't willing to share with me. I'm a bit of a control freak. It was incredibly hard to give him the space he needed when I so desperately wanted to orchestrate his life and smooth things out for him. I also missed him immensely and craved the connection, even if it was just a random text here and there.

Whether Zack called me routinely or not, shared all that was going on in his life or not, there was no doubt in my mind that I would move heaven and earth to get him whatever he needed—be it in an emergency or just for his well-being. I'm his mother. I'll always want to help him get what's best for him.

God is our loving Father and yearns to be involved in our lives too. There's nothing that brings Him more joy than for us to turn to Him and share all that we're experiencing. Not only does He have the perfect wisdom to guide us, but consistent connection with Him also gifts us with the promise in Matthew 13:16—eyes to see the love and peace He's offering us all the time.

Nevertheless, He doesn't keep score and will still rescue us and give us what's best for us even if we only turn to Him when we're in need. However, it's by remaining connected to Him that we maintain the eyes and ears to recognize His goodness in the here and now, and all the ways He's answered our prayers in the past.

Seek Him for Peace

So, if true peace is found in love, then we all have access to the one source: God. Let's stop seeking peace in comfort and, instead, seek peace in Him. Let's experience that head-over-heels love God is always offering us, a love that brings a deep and unwavering serenity if we'd just free-fall into it. Let's turn to Him, over and over again, building relationships and standing on His promise to always work for our good no matter how things appear on the surface. Let's stay in His Word where story after story reminds us just how faithful He is in providing that peace.

The following stories in this book illustrate the same. Each one is from an author who experienced firsthand how God is always offering peace, no matter the circumstances. They're proof that God is active in the here and now, every moment of every day, showering grace on any heart that remains open and faithful to Him. May these stories inspire you to see how God is always working for your good in ways you may only recognize when viewed through the eyes of faith.

A heart at peace gives life to the body, but envy rots the bones.

Proverbs 14:30 (NIV)

MY OWN AMAZING RACE

By Lynne Hartke

"ONE RUNNER," MY SON, Nate, said as he plopped down the $3 registration fee for his son, Micah, to participate in the community track meet.

Athletes of all ages surrounded us—from high school, middle school, and elementary. Eyes wide, Micah surveyed the oval track and infield. A hurdler practiced his rhythm as he sailed over a row of hurdles. A volunteer raked the gravel pit for the long jump. A coach gave pointers to a group of young girls as they stretched out their calf muscles on the grass.

At age three, Micah seemed out of place—more of a team mascot than a serious participant. Yet, despite his small stature, in his young chest beat the heart of a runner.

"Play chase, Grandma?" Micah had asked an hour earlier while his mom, Rachel, had organized camp chairs, water bottles, and snacks for the evening competition. Chase was Micah's favorite game.

I had chased Micah around the couch, the coffee table, and the dining room chairs, all while avoiding building blocks, stuffed animals, and the upheaval of life with two young children. His gray terrier barked in time with our pounding feet, as Micah switched directions and began chasing me. His toddler sister, Madelyn, joined in the fun, until we all had collapsed on the couch, laughing, while Micah begged for more.

• • •

A whirling dynamo of energy, Micah only knew one speed: running. From the minute his eyes popped open in the morning until the final second of his day, Micah was on the move. Desperate for an organized activity to harness all the energy, Nate and Rachel had signed Micah up at a local track meet, advertised for children of all ages. With no limitations on the number of events a racer could enter, Micah lined up at the starting line for the first event—the 100-meter dash.

As Nate helped him get in place, I noticed the words on Micah's shirt—*This Is What AMAZING Looks Like.* The words were not in pastel pink or pale yellow, but in bold red letters, like a fire engine racing down the highway.

The starting horn blew, and the group took off. Micah did not think about being amazing. He only focused on one thing.

Micah ran with his arms pumping and little legs hitting the ground, while all the older kids outdistanced him. When he finished in last place, he was not concerned, because he was participating in something he loved.

This Is What AMAZING Looks Like.

• • •

The message on the shirt sucker punched me in the chest. Amazing? When was the last time I felt amazing?

I had struggled with feelings of failure since opening an email from my agent the week before, an email I had assumed had contained good news. Instead, I had scanned the words in disbelief.

Your book proposal was not accepted.

Six simple words had spelled the death of a dream, the finish line to months of writing and research. How was it possible? I searched the email for clues.

It comes down to your platform and presence on social media. It is not big enough.

Although my agent had included words of encouragement, I had focused on those three words. *Not big enough. Not big enough.*

The words stomped like heavy footsteps on my dreams. In my own game of chase, I was outclassed and outperformed. To make matters worse—after the email from my agent—every social media post from friends and acquaintances had news of their accomplishments in their careers, relationships, and goals in life. A fellow writer received an award for her new novel. A friend earned a coveted new position at work. Another shared photo after photo of a vacation in Cancún.

Winning. Winning. Winning.

And me?

Amazing was the last thing I experienced until I wondered if it was even worth stepping up to the starting line any longer. I felt as squashed as the tarmac beneath the athletes' racing feet.

A loser. A loser with envy burning inside.

"Let's stand at the finish line so Micah can see us," Rachel said, as Micah stepped into place for the 200-meter run. Shaking off my sour mood, I grabbed the hand of toddler Madelyn, who was more interested in examining the grass at her feet than watching her brother.

"Go, Micah, go!" we screamed with other parents and grandparents as Micah ran—and finished last again.

This Is What AMAZING Looks Like.

Micah did the long jump. Tossed the javelin. His dad talked him out of running the mile.

"Runners, line up for the 4 x 100 relay." A volunteer shouted the words through a yellow megaphone as a desert sunset stained the sky.

Micah joined his team of three-year-old friends as he stepped onto the track in lane nine as the last runner, the anchor, for his team. His head reached the thighs of the older runner who stretched in the lane next to him. While his competitor sported the beginning of a mustache on his upper lip, Micah sported freckles and the biggest grin on his face, completely unaware that he was the shortest runner, with the littlest legs, and in the worst lane on the track. He didn't know he was not big enough.

The other runners received their batons and sprinted down the track. By the time Micah began running his leg of the relay, everyone else had finished the race.

"Hey! My grandson is still on the track!" I screamed, as athletes wandered across the lanes, picking up gear and duffle bags. Assuming the race was over, nobody noticed a three-year-old runner carrying a baton, the metal tube larger than his entire arm.

Nobody noticed.

Frustrated, I yelled the words again. Why didn't anyone see him?

I see him. And I see you.

• • •

The quiet words reverberated into the depths of me, not audible, but heard, nonetheless. I knew the words were spoken by Jesus, my Creator of my race.

I see you.

The commotion on the track faded as volumes of truth downloaded into my heart in a moment of time. In my own game of chase, trying to grasp amazing—amazing in the striving, in the endless to-do lists, and postponed dreams—I was known. Seen.

Loved.

Rather than enjoying my race, I had stepped on the endless treadmill of comparison, the myth of when-then. *When* I get a book contract, *then* I will be happy. *When* I make the *New York Times* Bestseller List, *then* I will be successful. The sourness in the pit of my stomach melted as I confessed my sin of envy and discontent. I did not need to compare my race to anyone else's.

"Clear the track," the announcer called after he finally spotted Micah in his red shirt coming down the straightaway.

Incredible peace filled my soul as I watched my grandson run. Legs pounding. Arms swinging. Hair bouncing to the cadence of each step. The entire crowd noticed as well. They saw a little boy who was still in the race, a tiny runner with *This Is What AMAZING Looks Like* shouting truth across his chest. A little boy who only loved to run.

In slow-motion unison, the crowd stood to their feet, clapping and shouting, along with me, Rachel, and Nate, "Go, go, go!"

Micah ran—all the way to the finish line, smiling huge, because it was a giant game of chase, and everyone was playing.

"Did you have fun?" Nate asked at the end of the event as he strapped Micah into his car seat for the drive home.

Micah nodded, grasping his blue ribbon, an award presented to him and his team as the only three-year-old participants. While the rest of us collapsed, exhausted, into the van, Micah had one more burning question.

"Dad?"

"Yes?"

"Can I run again tomorrow?"

Prayer for a Peace-Filled Life

Lord Jesus, when I am tempted to step on the treadmill of comparison, help me be content to run my own race as I keep my eyes on You. Amen.

Peace I leave with you; my peace I give you. I do not give to you as the world gives. Do not let your hearts be troubled and do not be afraid.

John 14:27 (NIV)

A TRAIN RIDE TO DACHAU

By Laurie Davies

THE LINE OF PEOPLE behind us growing in number and agitation, my husband and I fumbled our way through the ticket kiosk's automated prompts at *München Hauptbahnhof*, or Munich Central Station. With few euros and even less German speaking skills, I felt the hot sting of stress mounting as we tried to book rail passage. Shrill boarding announcements over the loudspeaker intensified the pressure.

Finally, mercifully, the kiosk dispensed our tickets. I looked sheepishly into the hot stares of passengers whose folded arms and furrowed brows had no language barrier.

Tickets in one hand and my son's hand in the other, we navigated the bustling, modern train station through a swirl of children on school trips, thirtysomethings in smart suits, and girlfriends ready to go take the town. Beads of perspiration dotted my forehead. By the time we worked our way past at least two dozen platforms, we found the number that matched the one on our tickets to our destination: the Dachau concentration camp.

We boarded our commuter train and I released a long sigh. I wondered if we shouldn't have just remained in Munich and taken the BMW factory tour instead. Sleek glass half panels created the feeling of a cocoon around my family's three-seat pod and the smooth lull of the train calmed my nerves.

• • •

This was the final day of our vacation. I hoped that ending it on such a somber note wouldn't ruin the whole thing. What was I looking for in a day trip to Dachau that I couldn't find in a history book? I stared out the window at lush trees, old barns, and the charred shell of a warehouse.

And then I saw it. A parallel train track.

Weathered wooden ties supported the tracks, which were long overgrown by grass and flowers. The significance of what we were doing hit me for the first time.

Could that have been the track that transported Jews, political opponents, priests, and others to the death camp during World War II? Instantly, what remained of my own stress dissolved, petty and pale compared with the terror that Dachau-bound families faced as they crammed into covered railcars bound for the cradle of Nazi dehumanization.

I looked at a spit-polished businessman, briefcase sitting next to his smart shoes, his copy of the newspaper *Süddeutsche Zeitung* snapped crisply in his hands. This looked like a normal commute for him, a young man who had learned secondhand about the horrors of Nazi Germany in history books just like me.

I surveyed the other passengers. Everyone seemed to be at ease, checking their phones, reading the news, nodding to sleep. Why didn't I feel any peace? How could the Prince of Peace even be present in the place we were visiting? Couldn't anyone see the emotional push-pull I'd gotten myself into? On one hand, I wanted my son to understand the reality of evil in this world. On the other hand, I wasn't sure I could bear to face it.

I checked my watch. If we hopped onto the southbound line, we might get back to Munich in time for the last tour at BMW.

• • •

My husband has known me more than half my life. When I cross one leg over the other, then unconsciously shift my weight and cross the other leg over the other—quickly back and forth, like a tic—he has learned it's time to hold my hand.

He pulled my hand into his. I squeezed it hard and stared down at the metal streak of those dormant railroad tracks.

We disembarked at the train station, and just like thousands of prisoners would have done in Dachau's twelve-year span of operation, we walked the nearly 2 miles to the death camp. We passed through the famed iron gates, greeted at eye level with the sardonic, iconic phrase: "*Arbeit macht frei*," German for "Work will set you free."

As the gate clanged closed behind us, I prayed quietly, softening the pointed question I had aimed at my Lord on the train: "Jesus, could you be the Prince of Peace in here today? Please?"

My family split up, deciding we wanted to see different things. I walked along a path where barracks built for a capacity of five thousand held an astonishing thirty thousand prisoners by the end of World War II.

I sat under the spectacle of unmanned watchtowers in the open sun next to what would have been the "medical" barracks, where human experimentation with hypothermia and pharmaceutical testing occurred. My eyes scanned the seemingly endless rows of barracks, or at least the footings that marked where the barracks had been. I imagined thousands of image bearers of God falling onto wood bunks in exhaustion following forced labor, dehumanization, and emaciation. I pictured their tears falling to the ground and their prayers piercing heaven. I wondered what this had done to God's heart.

I sat. Tears fell.

Had the Prince of Peace reigned at all in this place? Or had evil kept Him on the periphery, perhaps even a neighborhood beyond the two-story houses that directly overlooked a ghastly part of the camp that would have been in their plain view—a whipping post and stakes where prisoners were chained.

When He walked the earth, Jesus had promised to leave His peace with us. But more than seventy-five years after the horrific events occurred here, at a time when the country was far from war, could His peace possibly be here?

• • •

I rose to my feet and walked between rows of poplar trees, which created an elegant skyline along otherwise bland khaki buildings. The trees swayed in a suddenly sweeping October wind, almost in answer to my question. Their uniform bending to the breeze struck me as I realized His peace has always swayed hearts.

It did in the Apostle Paul, who endured shipwrecks, brutality, and imprisonment.

It did in the heart of Corrie Ten Boom after she forgave a Nazi guard who worked at the Ravensbrück death camp, where her sister died.

In my own lifetime, I'd watched peace rule in the heart of a friend who had offered months of bedside hospice care to the dying father who had sexually abused her as a child.

Jesus promised He would leave His peace with us. And in the simple sway of a poplar tree, I realized He doesn't dispense it like the world does. His peace has never relied on regimes. It doesn't need the backing of military might. His peace doesn't need a piece of paper, a fragile treaty that can be undone by the stroke of a pen or unhinged by a madman.

His peace penetrates all the way into the heart.

I counted on that promise as I had one more stop to make. Dread, guilt, and curiosity's obligation compelled me past gnarled coils of barbed wire to the compound's crematorium, where evil, coal, and human beings had fueled body-length ovens. I locked eyes with a tourist from France and we shared enough language to express that neither of us could stay in that room.

Retreating into the main camp, I made my way back to the poplar trees. They seemed the only oasis in this otherwise desperate place.

I exited through the "*Arbeit macht frei*" gate, swinging it open as wide as the screeching hinge would allow. I let it clang shut and sat on a concrete platform next to the set of railroad tracks used for shipping goods to the camp.

The screech-clang, screech-clang pattern punctuated my thoughts and I was glad to see my husband and son approaching the gate. I walked toward them, listened for one more screech-clang as they exited, and gazed in at the swaying poplars one more time.

I hadn't noticed it earlier. The leaves were rippling.

Gravel crunched under our feet as we left the grounds. I prayed that peace would ripple in the hearts and minds of the visitors we passed. I gave God thanks that His peace is not a politically expedient promise or a feeling that changes with the wind.

I heard what God had whispered to me through the poplars that day. I understood that His peace is an inside job.

Prayer for a Peace-Filled Life

Lord, even when our circumstances and our environment defy peace, help us remember that the peace of Christ can reign in our hearts no matter where we are.

May the God of hope fill you with all joy and peace as you trust in him, so that you may overflow with hope by the power of the Holy Spirit.

Romans 15:13 (NIV)

THE SOLACE OF SUNFLOWERS

By Tamara Bundy

SEVERAL YEARS AGO, I had the honor of helping a dear friend, Father Jim Willig, write a book about his cancer battle and all he was being taught in the throes of his two-year fight.

During his illness, a gentleman once commented that Father Jim was like a sunflower. Father Jim laughed at this suggestion. "I like sunflowers," he said, "but can't I be something strong and sturdy like a mighty oak?"

The man answered, "A sunflower never takes its face away from the sun, where it gets its strength. It also leaves behind multiple seeds that continue to grow and bloom long after what appears to be a too-short life."

Father Jim was touched by this analogy and understood. The name stuck, and he was forever labeled our Sunflower Priest.

• • •

So many people prayed for our beloved Sunflower Priest, who indeed lived his life never taking his eyes off the Son, in whom he found strength. And when Father Jim passed away at the age of fifty, several of us struggled to find the reason. It was hard to watch this amazing servant of the Lord suffer so and be taken from us at such a young age. I confess to a deep sadness, even a doubt in how the death of a young, inspiring man could be a part of God's perfect plan.

Shortly after Father Jim's funeral, I was wallowing in this doubt. He had been a mentor and a friend to me. He made me want to be a better person. I simply could not be around Father Jim without wanting a closer walk with Jesus. But my Sunflower Priest was gone, and I admit, my faith was badly shaken. That's when I received my first sunflower.

• • •

While running an errand at a local mall, I parked my car and stepped out into the stifling air of a July day. Without paying much attention to anything but the heat beating down on my grief, I walked as if on autopilot toward the store where I was headed. Somehow, and for a reason I can't explain, I glanced down.

There, right at my left foot, in the middle of a blacktopped parking lot, a sunflower was growing—a perfect sunflower!

My heart beat a little faster. How did that get there? Why was it in the middle of the parking lot?

I looked around for a flower shop or anything that might explain a sunflower appearing there on this hot summer day. But there was nothing. It made absolutely no sense that a random sunflower was right there, right then.

And yet, that surprise sunflower made perfect sense as my grieving soul understood more than my head possibly could. That sunflower spoke God's words to my hurting heart as loudly as if it were a burning bush. And my head began to understand too. I felt joy where there had been sadness. I felt hope where doubt had taken up residency. I felt at peace for the first time in a long time.

And that was only the beginning.

• • •

Over the next twenty years, I would continue to have moments of missing my inspiring friend, even as I grew to better understand how the seeds of the ministry he left behind continued to grow in glory and service to the Lord. That book I was blessed to write with him, *Lessons from the School of Suffering*, would go on to be translated into four languages, allowing Father Jim to continue preaching God's Word long after he left this earth. I continued to be blessed by Father Jim as well.

Gratefully, I would also continue receiving sunflowers, always appearing around the anniversary of his death. Some of these were easily explained as friends and family who knew my attachment to this special flower would gift them to me. But the arrival of some of my sunflowers appeared to be nothing less than heaven-sent.

Like this past summer.

My husband and I had moved to a new home the year before. The previous owners were not landscapers, and our new yard was basically bare. Very few flowers were planted there, and the one we searched for was not anywhere around.

I'm sure it might have made sense to run out and buy my seeds to guarantee the appearance of my special sunflowers. But I didn't. I can't say it was a conscious decision to wait and be surprised, but I think deep down I had hope. I believed. And God didn't disappoint.

• • •

As spring rolled around and the earth finally thawed, I noticed something growing next to our house where nothing was the year before. It was a simple sprout that I suspected was a weed. Still, I left it growing there admittedly more out of laziness than great faith. For once, my laziness was not a bad thing.

I didn't have to wait too long to see the telltale signs of a sunflower growing where nothing had been. Soon the beautiful bud hinted at a flower that would be beyond any I had seen. When it finally bloomed, I felt that same rush of joy and hope that I felt every year. I ran to get my husband to show him the plant that held such promise for me. He pointed out something that, in my excitement, I hadn't yet realized: My surprise sunflower bloomed on the exact anniversary of the Sunflower Priest's birth into his eternal life.

There would end up being three sunflowers that year that grew over 6 feet tall. Every day, I would talk to those sunflowers, thanking them for coming to me, thanking God for His gifts that go (and grow) beyond our greatest comprehension. My heart can now celebrate the full story of Father Jim's life and death as I praise Jesus for the gift of the seeds the Sunflower Priest left behind that continue to grow.

I still miss my friend. Somedays when I am in a mellow mood, I wonder what inspiration he would give the world right now if he had been blessed with the fervently prayed-for healing and a long life. But the message of the surprise sunflowers always returns to me, eventually flooding my soul with the joy and peace of God's faithfulness, leading me to glorify Him for hopeful beginnings that grow out of painful endings.

Prayer for a Peace-Filled Life

Lord, when I get overwhelmed with the grief and disappointment of today, help me turn my eyes from my own sadness and frustration and instead focus on You. Remind me of the seeds of Your miracles that sprout throughout my life.

For anyone who enters God's rest also rests from their works, just as God did from his.

Hebrews 4:10 (NIV)

THE PROMISE AND PRACTICE OF REST

By Eryn Lynum

IT WAS THE FIRST DAY of January and the first Saturday of the year, when my husband, four children, and I began practicing Sabbath. We awoke to a fresh blanket of snow outside, and everything felt new, including Sabbath. Of course, God's promise of rest was not new. He had set an example in Genesis 2:3 (NIV) when He rested after His work of creation: "Then God blessed the seventh day and made it holy, because on it he rested from all the work of creating that he had done."

I saw God's promise of rest in the New Testament when I read Hebrews 4:9 (NIV): "There remains, then, a Sabbath-rest for the people of God." No, it wasn't this long-standing practice that was new. Instead, my perspective of God's rest was renewed, like a landscape covered by fresh snow.

Staring out the window on our first family Sabbath, I watched black-capped chickadees collecting seeds from our feeders. Their morning routines echo Psalm 104:13 (NIV): "The land is satisfied with the fruit of his work." I'd recently learned that Sabbath, stemming from the Hebrew word *Shabbat*, can mean "stop and delight." Could I practice God's example of stopping and delighting? Could I set aside my toilsome work and, like the chickadees, find satisfaction in the fruit of God's work? I was determined to try.

• • •

Before I could accept God's gift of rest, I had to determine what had been keeping me from it. What was unrestful? I began naming whatever was a barrier to rest: Checking emails. Driving in traffic. Spending money. Reading and responding to text messages. Notifications on my phone. As I named these obstacles to rest, I also identified what is conducive to rest: Reading. Watching birds. Walking outside. Playing chess with my kids. Journaling by hand. Sipping tea. In creating these lists, I found I had to deconstruct my habits and get back to the basics of rest.

Even then, resting felt uncomfortable at first, like an itchy sweater on a chilly day. The television remained off, and our phones were silenced and tucked into drawers. Our kids weren't sure where to direct their boredom. Yet without much prompting, that boredom gave way to imaginative play outside in the wintry landscape. Meanwhile, I was determined to read a book again—training my attention to the words in front of me. I read until I lost track of time.

As we created new habits throughout the following weeks, I discovered that I must fight for rest. In Hebrews 4:11 (ESV) I read, "Let us therefore strive to enter that rest." I don't naturally connect the concepts of striving and rest. Yet Scripture makes it clear that rest is something I must work toward—especially when stopping and taking a break goes against everything our culture demands.

I had to strip down the misconceptions that society had planted in my mind. Rest is not lazy—it is biblical. Over time and practice, I would even find that resting one day a week infused the other six days with greater creativity and productivity. Rooted in rest, my week is more fruitful.

• • •

That first family Sabbath was a beautiful glimpse of what God was beginning in our hearts and home. Like a seed in fragrant soil, God's promise germinates and is nurtured by His grace, eventually growing to full fruition in our souls. He was tilling the soil in our home, breaking up hard ground, and preparing us to receive His promise.

When the kids barreled in the front door, shaking snow from boots and with their noses and cheeks flushed red, I set milk to warm on the stove for hot chocolate. After a quick break to warm up, our kids eagerly bounded back outdoors—this time with my husband and me. Geared up in our snow pants, hats, and gloves, we enjoyed a leisurely walk. Without anywhere else to be, we stopped to chat with neighbors. Our four-year-old daughter sat contentedly in the sled my husband pulled behind him. Listening to the kids' laughter meld with songs from resident birds braving the winter, I couldn't believe that this would now be one-seventh of our lives moving forward.

As we've practiced setting aside the busyness of our weeks and accepting God's promised rest, it feels like we are redeeming time. There were many years of my life when I failed to receive God's rest. But what matters now is that moving forward, we are choosing differently. And my past efforts are an integral part of my journey into God's rest.

My attempts at Sabbath have been many, stretching back to my high school years. When I was sixteen, I took my first job working in a café. I explained to my manager that I would need a regular day of rest, and he reluctantly agreed I could take every Friday off. Looking back, I wonder what he thought about this request. As a grown professional with a career, did he perceive my youthful energy and question why a sixteen-year-old would need to rest? Reflecting back a decade and a half later, I wonder the same. As my husband and I raise and homeschool four children and run three businesses, I'm tempted to look back at my teenage self and laugh. I thought I needed rest back then?

But I did—just as I do now. God supplies sufficient rest for each of life's seasons. My need for His rest is not dialed up or down depending on how hectic my days are.

I don't earn God's gift of rest by working hard. Rather, it's a promise available to me no matter my season of life. In fact, it has nothing to do with my accomplishments—but everything to do with what Christ has accomplished on my behalf.

In Hebrews 4, I began to grasp the connection between God's rest and Christ's finished work on the cross. Only as I practice believing everything Christ has done for me can I enter God's promise of rest. His rest is far greater than a nap in the shade or a break from the monotony of work. It is a deep soul rest only He can provide.

• • •

God invited my family deeper into Sabbath over each consecutive Saturday. He drew me into a profound understanding of rest and belief and how they are interconnected. I read in Hebrews 4:3 (NIV), "Now we who have believed enter that rest," and then in verse 6 (KJV), "And they to whom it was first preached entered not in because of unbelief." I had to ask myself, when have I failed to enter God's rest because of my unbelief?

As I accept and believe all Christ has accomplished on my behalf, I am liberated from my endless striving. I can live a life defined by His rest! I can stop and delight because God is my great provider.

My commitment to Sabbath rest has ebbed and flowed over the years. I often default back to busyness. I have been like those mentioned in Isaiah 28:12 (ESV), to whom God said, "'This is rest; give rest to the weary; and this is repose'; yet they would not hear."

However, this past year of practicing the Sabbath as a family has been different. I no longer see Sabbath as an unrealistic command that I can't live up to. Instead, God is removing my guilt around failed attempts. I am viewing Sabbath as He intends it: as a gift. We can take it or leave it. And our family, with an ever-increasingly busy calendar, can no longer afford to leave it.

Embracing Sabbath is an act of faith in my life. Every time I put away my work for a day, I am trusting God to provide for our family. When I trade Saturday afternoon errands for a slow day with my family, I trust God that there is enough of what I need right at home. Tucking my phone away, I trust there are meaningful connections to be enjoyed with the people right in front of me. When I flip the page on our calendar and fill it up with activities for the month but choose to reserve one day a week for rest, I trust that He gives ample time to get everything done in six days. Whenever I observe the Sabbath, God's promise of rest roots deeper into my being.

Prayer for a Peace-Filled Life

Dear God, I accept Your promise of rest. Help me to set aside work and distractions as an act of faith and experience the soul-deep rest only You can give.

"Martha, Martha," the Lord answered, "you are worried and upset about many things . . . Mary has chosen what is better, and it will not be taken away from her."

Luke 10:41–42 (NIV)

WHEN WORRY AND DISTRACTION unite, they become thieves that rob us of peace. It happens most when we take on too much or when we take on a task with the wrong intention, neglecting to do it from the heart. We feel the ramifications of the overwhelm or disconnect throughout our body: A tension headache sets in that won't let up. We grind our teeth at night and wake with a throbbing jaw. There's a constant, dull ache in the pit of our stomach. Worse yet, worry and tension shield our heart like armor, deflecting any semblance of peace.

It happened to Martha when Jesus came to dinner with the disciples. Initially, her desire to serve a meal worthy of the Son of God was most likely rooted in good intention. As her sister, Mary, sat at the Lord's feet, Martha's need to take on too much stole her focus, leading her straight to the feet of worry and distraction, where she was no longer able to serve from the heart. Looking around at all she still needed to do, panic set in and told her she couldn't accomplish it all.

We, too, are prone to losing our way in the fast-paced world we live in. We want to do it all and do it to the best of our ability—no matter what "it" is. We rarely draw boundaries. We rarely say no. Even if our hearts are in the right place when we initially say yes, the juggling act becomes so overwhelming it leads our heart astray. Once our head and our heart are misaligned, we're left susceptible to anxiety, self-pity, resentment, and more. That's the time we need to hear the same words Jesus said to Martha: "Mary has chosen what is better, and it will not be taken away."

His words aren't a rebuke, like some people interpret them. They're a soothing invitation to leave the striving behind, and a promise that if we spend time at His feet, listening to all He has to say, our stress and tension will dissolve. What's more, they're replaced by His peace that cannot be taken away.

—Claire McGarry

For this reason a man will leave his father and mother and be united to his wife, and the two will become one flesh. . . . Therefore what God has joined together, let no one separate.

Mark 10:7–9 (NIV)

UNSEVERED COMMITMENT

By Claire McGarry

WHEN I WAS A KID, my grandparents lived in Boston. They were city people through and through. Neither of them had a driver's license nor a car. They didn't need to. The streetcar could take them wherever they needed to go. I loved visiting them in their home that had so many spaces to discover. As my mother sat at the kitchen table, having "adult conversation" with them over a cup of tea, I'd spend my time exploring their house and all the memorabilia my grandfather had collected and stored in the basement.

As time went by and my grandparents grew older, they were less able to travel about on the streetcar. Simultaneously, crime was increasing in the city, making it dangerous to live there. I was thrilled when my uncle Charlie moved them to suburbia, into a home right up the street from ours. Now I could walk to their house by myself and spend more time with them. Always wanting to take piano lessons, but never having a piano, they offered me theirs to use. I began practicing on it every day and using it for my weekly lessons with my teacher. I'd always stay afterwards, doing whatever chores Gramma and Pop needed and then sitting and visiting with them.

Gramma was very hard of hearing. She set up camp in the living room, where she could blast her "stories" (soap operas) as loud as she needed to. Pop, needing to "escape that racket," set up camp in the four-season porch, where he could watch *Jeopardy!* and his crime shows in peace.

They never let that distance separate them, though. Pop would leave the sliding glass door to the porch open so they could yell back and forth to each other throughout the course of the day. Pop didn't just yell at top volume so Gramma could hear him. Yelling had become his default from working at a noisy bar all of his adult life. An outsider would have said his voice had an edge of impatience, but those of us who knew them had learned that shouting was their love language. When you listened between the words, you could hear a profound connection that no bickering could ever sever.

• • •

They'd been married for over sixty-one years. Having gone to the same school and church as kids, they knew each other for years before marrying. In fact, they married in secret, fearful Gramma's mother wouldn't approve because they were so young. After a quick honeymoon at a local beach, Gramma actually returned to her mother's house, trying to keep the marriage covert. My great-grandmother was savvier than that, though. She knew they'd married, exchanging their vows before God, and she also knew when she'd been beaten. She reluctantly blessed the marriage and allowed them to live together.

As a married couple, they worked as a team to raise their growing family. Pop's income tending bar and playing the accordion in an Irish band didn't stretch far enough to feed and clothe their eight children. So, Gramma spent her nights cleaning the dorms at the local colleges and eventually moved on to cleaning hospital rooms throughout the city. What they lacked in finances, they made up for in other ways. Theirs was a home filled with laughter, music, and faith. Jesus was the cornerstone they built their family upon, and faith is what got them through each crisis.

The Wall Street Crash of 1929 taught them how to be creative and stretch a penny even farther than they ever thought possible. World War II taught them that the only way to remain strong with two sons in the military was to entwine their hearts even tighter with constant prayer. The Korean and Vietnam wars taught them that peace was worth fighting for, even if it meant four more of their sons enlisting in the military. In truth, Gramma loved the United States so much that she would have encouraged her sons to enlist whether there were wars to be fought or not. She thought it was critical for them to learn love of country firsthand and recognize that freedom is never free.

• • •

When peace finally did seem to be something they could count on, the rug was pulled out from under them when Pop had a cerebral hemorrhage. Hearing that he only had two hours to live, Gramma gathered their eight grown children and their spouses around his bedside. She fervently led the prayers that would alter his prognosis and see him live another twenty-seven years. For his part, Pop pounded the gates of heaven every time his Peg's chronic heart condition flared up. With every heart attack and extended hospital stay she had, Pop's prayers made it perfectly clear to God that it wasn't time to take her yet.

When two of their sons had heart attacks before they were forty, Gramma and Pop united their prayers at a volume God couldn't ignore, and both men made it through. Without a doubt, every hardship my grandparents faced fused them closer, taking their faith and commitment to a whole new level, one that seemed to reach the heavens.

As I spent time at their house each afternoon, I got to witness that commitment in action. Gramma didn't approve of alcohol, yet she knew how much Pop enjoyed a drink at night. That single highball she placed at his seat for dinner was an outward sign of how she always put his wants before her own. Despite Gramma wearing a housecoat every day, Pop would always find a way to show her he still thought she was beautiful. Whether it was a random compliment he'd toss into his shouting or a tender touch he'd make in passing, Pop let Gramma know she was still as pretty as the day they'd married. Nothing was effusive, but those subtle statements of love were loud and clear.

• • •

When I went off to college years later, I looked forward to breaks when I'd get to see them again. Just weeks into my sophomore year, however, the phone rang. It was a Wednesday morning at 9:30. Before I even said hello, I somehow knew it was my mother, telling me Gramma had passed away. I immediately went home and stayed with Pop for the week. He did his best to hold up during the services, but when everyone was gone, he was a different person. It was as if he were only half there, off-balance, unable to stand straight without his other half. Three weeks later to the day, my phone rang again at college. It was a Wednesday at 9:30 a.m. Once more, I knew before answering it that it was my mother, telling me Pop had passed away.

It seems all those years before, when they'd stood before God in secret and made a vow to live as one, my grandparents wove that promise around both their hearts and deep into their souls. When one went up to heaven on a Wednesday, that cord of love wasn't torn. Instead, it gently pulled the other one up on another Wednesday so they could continue to live as one in the direct presence and peace of God.

Prayer for a Peace-Filled Life

God of Everlasting Love, thank You for the loving couples who teach us what true commitment looks like. May they all be reunited in You, where true peace is found. Amen.

The LORD gives strength to his people; the LORD blesses his people with peace.

Psalm 29:11 (NIV)

HEALED AT SEA

By Elsa Kok Colopy

MY HANDS WERE SHAKING when I hung up the phone, adrenaline coursing through my veins. I hurried over to the computer and started looking up flights.

"What's going on?" My coworker Jan asked. She could see I was shaken. "Elsa, what's happening?"

I heard myself say the words, but I still couldn't believe them. "My dad is missing. He went for a sail this morning and they just discovered his boat. It had run aground and no one was onboard. I have to get to Florida. Now! I have to find him!"

Jan came over and put her hand on my shoulder. "Oh, Elsa. I'm so sorry. What can I do?"

"Can you let our boss know? And maybe give me a ride home?"

"Done." She hurried off while I finished booking the next available flight.

• • •

I tried to imagine what could have happened. My dad, a true Dutchman, had been sailing since he was just a little boy. Even though he was eighty-two, he still went out nearly every day to explore the inland waterways near his Floridian home. Maybe his boat got away from him somehow. Maybe he was even now standing on an island, cursing up a storm as it floated off. Surely this was all just a mere annoyance, nothing worse. *Please, Lord.*

I gathered up my belongings and hopped in my friend's car. It was a short drive home, and as we pulled in, my phone rang again.

"Elsa, he's gone."

"I know, Mom. I'm coming to help find him!"

"No, Elsa, he's gone." Sobs nearly swallowed up her next words. "They found his body."

Time seemed to stand still. No, it couldn't be. *Not my dad. No. Please.*

"Can you call your brothers?"

As the youngest girl with four older brothers, I dreaded telling my siblings. We were all so close. Their reaction was as I imagined. Anguish. Sorrow. A series of "I'm not ready for this!" and heartfelt cries.

We traveled from all over the country and arrived on my mom's doorstep, hearts heavy and burdened. The first hours, we just held and hugged each other, shocked at this turn of events. Eventually we started talking, and my mom explained what she knew. It had been a normal morning.

Dad had called out to her as he headed off for his sail, "I'll see you later!" He boated out of the small marina and went on his way. Normally he stayed in the inland waterways, but on this occasion, he must have been feeling brave. He had ventured out onto the open ocean. He didn't do that often, but the calm winds that day must have lured him out. Witnesses said he slowly went through the inlet and motored out onto the glassy water.

We don't know exactly what happened next, only that a lifeguard spotted his boat coming toward the public beach. The lifeguard honked his air horn and called out via his megaphone, warning my dad that he was coming into an area with people. But the boat did not stop. When it ran aground, the lifeguard called out and eventually went on board. No one was there. He immediately called the authorities and the coast guard sent up a plane. That's when they found my dad, 4 miles out to sea. He had drowned. They speculated he had tumbled overboard while walking to the bow to adjust some rigging. He didn't have the best balance, so we could almost envision that scenario in our minds.

"What a miracle they found his body," some said.

Yes, I thought, *but he is still gone.*

"Good that the boat ran aground instead of going out to sea!" others said. "At least you have closure."

Yes, but he is still gone.

We couldn't help thinking about his final moments. Was he scared? Did he panic? Did he think about us? If he had fallen, was he conscious when he went into the water? What a horrible feeling, wondering and not knowing, imagining him alone out there in the cold ocean as the boat moved away from him.

• • •

Because my dad loved the water from an early age, it seemed fitting that we would scatter his ashes out to sea. We decided to rent a large boat so we could go together. We brought along roses for each adult child and grandchild to leave on the water as well. After a moving service, we gathered and set out for the inlet. My mom said a few words and we watched as she poured out his ashes, the gray dust coloring the water as it slowly began to sink. Each of us dropped a rose upon the swath of gray, leaving a trail of red behind our boat.

It was after we scattered his ashes and placed roses in the water that we spotted them—dolphins playing in the distance. My dad had always loved dolphins, seemed to be friends with them on his sails. They would often come beside his boat and playfully frolic alongside. We'd heard many the story of his interactions with them.

I was standing at the bow of the boat when I saw them, chills running up and down my arms. They came closer. Closer still. The dolphins came all the way to the boat where we all stood. They led the boat for several moments before veering off and playfully back again. We all gasped and laughed and cried. So fitting that the dolphins would come to say goodbye as well.

Had they been there all along? It felt right to imagine Dad had companions for his final moments, the same companions who had been with him day after day on his sails. Why wouldn't they be with him through the end? Protecting him until his body was found? As we watched the dolphins dance along the bow and side of the boat, a divine comfort fell over our hearts.

If God used dolphins to bring us comfort, we reasoned, surely He used dolphins to be with Dad in his final breaths.

Peace flooded our hearts as laughter filled the air.

The dolphins trailed away, leaving joy in their wake.

Thank You, Lord.

Prayer for a Peace-Filled Life

God, thank You for being my comfort and peace! You orchestrate all of creation to pour out Your love to me. Help me to keep my eyes fixed on You. Amen.

And the peace of God, which transcends all understanding, will guard your hearts and your minds in Christ Jesus.

Philippians 4:7 (NIV)

BEYOND UNDERSTANDING

By Heather Jepsen

I APPROACH GOD differently than other pastors I know. I've always been a bit skeptical when it comes to God's action in our world. How can we study and understand God while also relying on our faith to lead us to the truth? This question was put to the test when I was a student in seminary.

I was in my twenties when my grandmother died. I was at her bedside, and instead of being filled with fear and grief, I was overwhelmed with joy. My grandma had suffered with various health concerns in her final years, and I was relieved that her suffering was over. When I witnessed her take her last breaths, I was certain she was traveling to heaven.

At that time in my life I didn't believe in a heaven, so my conviction that this was where Grandma was going was strange. I wrestled with this certainty of heart as it warred with a certainty of mind. Finally, my mind gave in, and I sincerely sought God. When I turned my heart to God in faith in a moment of honest prayer, I witnessed a vision, and I heard a voice. God told me I was loved, and God told me I was going to be a pastor. I was called to share God's love with the world.

While I was confident in my heart that this call was from God, I struggled to give in to it. My will was strong, and I was young. I wanted to live my life like other young kids do, going to bars and having fun. I didn't want to be a pastor; I wanted to be young and free. It took me years of internal struggle to finally answer God's call and go to seminary. I thought I could work around this call somehow or ignore God.

When I finally gave in to going to seminary to be trained for ministry, I still rebelled against the call of God. I cut my hair short, I got a tattoo, and I drank more than I should. The school I attended was in the San Francisco Bay Area, which seemed like a perfect place to party and have fun. The other young students in my class and I often went into the city to check out the scene in various neighborhoods. During the weeks we would study and go to class, but on the weekends we would drink and party. It seemed I wasn't the only one rebelling against the God who had marked me for service.

The class that finally turned me around was theology. Theology is the study of religious belief and theory. Rather than focusing strictly on the Scripture, this class was about why we believe what we believe about God. This was the place to ask questions about the divine—and I had so many questions. Why do we suffer? Why is there pain? Why did Jesus have to die? And why did God call me? I struggled to focus as my mind reeled with all the new material.

I failed my first test. In all my years of education, I had never gotten an F. My professor took me aside after class. "I can see your struggle," he said. "Let's meet in my office and talk about it later this week." He walked me through the test I had failed and as we discussed each question, he realized that I did understand the material. I knew the answers to the questions, I just couldn't explain them when I wrote them out. It was like there was a block between my pen, my mind, and my heart.

What was I going to do? I was never going to understand this God! I was ready to give up on the whole thing altogether. But, of course, God was working behind the scenes to keep me safe and on the right path. God had chosen me for ministry, and He was not going to let me mess that up.

First, I stopped drinking. I realized that I could not fight my way through seminary, and I let go of my inner sense of rebellion. I needed to trust God to carry me through the process and that meant I needed to have a clear head.

The second change was falling in love. There was a young man at the seminary who was just as much of an odd fit as I was. Often when I was in my dorm room studying, I would see him riding by outside on his Rollerblades. Back and forth, back and forth, until finally he would knock on my door. He wanted to go for a hike in the woods or a walk on the beach. Lars was such a calming presence. He didn't know me before seminary, so he didn't expect me to be anyone other than who I was. He believed that God called me to ministry, and he encouraged me to answer that call. Two years later we would get married.

• • •

As the spring semester wore on, I continued to try to settle in and find peace in my call. I finally let God be in charge as I sought answers to my questions. I stopped trying to understand everything with my mind and started letting some things just be based on faith in my heart. I continued to struggle in my theology class, and I ended up taking oral examinations instead of written ones so I could prove I knew the material. I excelled in all my other courses, but in theology there continued to be a disconnect. Something about the study of God just didn't click with me.

When the term ended, I struggled to prepare for the final exam. How was I going to explain everything I had learned about God? How could I even explain God at all? So much of my knowledge of God simply lived in my heart. It was a deep knowing, beyond the understanding of my mind. Eventually that is what gave me peace. But first, I needed to answer all the questions on the test.

The day came, and with some struggle, I made it through. I got a B in the class, and I was very proud of that B. I could not answer all the questions I had about God. And I still wasn't certain which theories from class I personally believed in and which I thought were a step too far. Through the coursework, I understood what other people believed about God, but I still struggled to find my own position. I think that was my difficulty. What did I really believe? And how could my heart of faith and my mind seeking understanding ever come together in union?

• • •

It's been over twenty years since I finished seminary and began my career as a pastor, and I still wonder just who God is. I have learned a lot more about God from my church experience than I ever learned from a professor in class. He is mystery and wonder, always here and yet also far away. God is someone we can struggle to grasp and understand, but also someone we will never fully know. God is right beside us and just out of reach all the time.

I have come to a deep sense of peace about God. I don't need to understand the whys of the world to have faith in the depths of my heart. I have found peace, not in letting go of my questions, but in letting go of the need to find all the answers. God is real, God is with us, and God is here. That is all we need to know. In that, I find peace.

Prayer for a Peace-Filled Life

God, help me to feel the truth of Your presence in my heart and find peace in my questioning mind. I don't have to understand You to believe in You.

There is no fear in love. But perfect love drives out fear, because fear has to do with punishment. The one who fears is not made perfect in love.

1 John 4:18 (NIV)

PERFECT LOVE

By Tara Johnson

SOMETIMES, moms just know.

They know when all isn't as it should be. When the other four-year-olds are able to count to ten but their child can't articulate "one," "two," or "three." Moms know it's strange when their four-year-old son can't ask for a specific food when he's hungry, but instead opens his mouth and grunts.

She knows something is wrong when her adorable little boy is four and she's still not heard him say his own name. She knows.

I knew.

Well-meaning friends told me not to worry. After all, my fun-loving bundle of energy had two big sisters who could speak for him. Why did he need to talk? He just hadn't found the *need* to that often. Others told me to chill. He's a boy. They don't mature as quickly as girls. Girls count numbers early, learn the alphabet, solve world peace, and knit blankets for their future husbands, while boys play in dirt and pick their noses. Nothing to worry about. Right?

I knew, but I didn't say much. Nate was healthy and extremely happy. A handsome boy with mischievous brown eyes, heart-melting dimples, and chestnut curls. He made friends easily and was always smiling. But still, there was something...

When the speech delay could no longer be ignored, we had him tested just before Christmas. The results came back for our little guy...severe cognitive delay paired with a severe speech delay.

• • •

As I sat at the tiny elementary school table, my legs tucked up under the too-small chair, I listened to the therapists lay out all the options for my son. I was calm. I knew God had gone before us and I knew none of this had taken Him by surprise. The therapists told me, from what they'd observed, they believed Nate could catch up over time.

And then came the words I had feared.

"Oh, and it might be time to test for autism."

I listened to their concerns, nodding in agreement, but my thoughts spun in dizzying circles. A thousand what-ifs tumbled through my mind. What would happen to my curious little boy? What kind of life would he have? Would he be bullied for being different? On and on the worries spun until the icy tentacles squeezing my heart grabbed me by the throat.

After our lengthy visit, Nate and I walked out to the car and I carefully tucked him into his car seat, my worries stacking up higher than Everest.

What if, what if, what if...

I drove away from the school with a heart too jumbled for examination. As we approached a red light, my tears finally broke free.

This was not how I imagined my son's life playing out.

"Monny!"

I looked back in the rearview mirror and Nate was grinning his big toothy grin at me, his brown eyes sparkling, one chubby hand waving.

"Hi, baby." I swiped at the hot tears running in streams down my face.

"Monny, sing Jee-Jee."

I sighed. Nate loved singing praise songs to Jesus (aka Jee-Jee), but my heart was too bruised, my voice thready and weak. Shaking my head, I tried to avert my gaze and took another swipe at my messy face. "Mommy can't right now, sweetie. I'm too sad."

Silence stretched. Then my heart tumbled as my son lifted up his sweet voice.

"Jee-Jee love me. Jee-Jee mine, Jee-Jee mine, Jee-Jee mine..."

I sucked in a breath. Was my nearly nonverbal child lifting up praise to his Creator? I blinked away the tears blurring my eyes. And my son didn't stop. His simple song continued as trees blurred past.

"Jee-Jee love me. Jee-Jee mine..."

Here I was, worrying over things I had no control over and the source of my angst was lifting up praises to Jesus. And in a flash, I understood.

For years, I'd wrestled with the verse "Perfect love casts out fear." I had dwelled on 1 John 4:18 (ESV) over and over until I could quote it verbatim. "There is no fear in love. But perfect love drives out fear, because fear has to do with punishment. The one who fears is not made perfect in love." But I still didn't understand it.

To get rid of fear, I need perfect love. Got it. But when I'm faced with a scary diagnosis, bills that keep piling up, rebellious loved ones, and a life that too easily spins out of control, I realize I have no idea what "perfect love" means.

I had bugged my pastor about it. Read commentaries and studied Bible languages. The Greek word for "drives" or "casts" has to do with a violent displacement. It means love grabs fear by the throat and throws it through the window. Descriptive. But what exactly is "perfect love"? Is it God's love for us? Our love for Him? The idea was murky, as if I was circling around the heart of the matter but couldn't grasp it.

Yet the moment my son lifted his tiny voice to sing, I understood.

The Bible repeatedly tells us Jesus is love. Perfect in every way.

Perfect love casts out fear.

• • •

Perfect love is Jesus, God wrapped in human flesh. Perfect love goes to any length to save and any height to reach. Perfect love calls the prisoner His brother, redeems him, and sets him free. Perfect love is complete, all consuming, with no traces of doubt in the power of the Holy One. Perfect love sets a glittering crown on the head of the orphan and calls him "Beloved." It sees no labels, no mistakes, no what-ifs.

The source of our praise, the One we worship is Jesus Christ. Fear cannot exist in His presence. It scatters like darkness shattered by light. Revelation twisted my heart with a surge of joy.

I pushed down the stinging tears and smiled. "Good idea, buddy. Let's praise Jesus."

We sang song after song on the car ride home. With each melody, my fear evaporated. Why? Because fear dissolves in the presence of praise.

Since that day in the car, few things have changed. Nate was officially diagnosed with autism, but he's the same awesome bundle of energy and joy he's always been, both before the diagnosis and after. The main thing that shifted was my perspective.

Going through this journey with my son has been incredibly rewarding. He works so hard to master new skills and concepts each week, but here's the thing—he's not worried about trying to make anybody happy or doing things the "right" way. He just loves life, learning, and people. And Nate has taught me how to celebrate the small things.

After his very first speech session, his amazing speech therapist, Susan, or "Miss Su-Su" as he calls her, led him out of the room with a big smile on her face.

"Nate, do you want to show Mommy what we learned today?"

He nodded and smiled.

Susan asked, "What's your name?"

He moved his fingers down his arm and tapped his wrist. "Nat-uh!" Perfect smile. Perfect joy. And perfect tears on this Mommy's part. In the last few years, those small victories have turned into big victories for our little guy.

• • •

And I've learned that not only is love perfect, but it's also sticky. I've pondered the best way to describe it for years and that's the best adjective I can use. Sticky. It won't let go. It clings. No matter the condition, grace stays, refusing to let go or give up. It extends love and blessings over and over again.

My son and I often play a little game called "Would You Love Me Even Then?" One of us asks the other if we would still love each other if crazy things altered our appearance, personality, or situation. Nate asks me questions like, "Mom, what if my hair was made out of spaghetti? Would you love me even then?" "What if my toes were made of hot dogs? Would you love me even then?" I assure him my love will never change, spaghetti hair or hot dog toes notwithstanding.

I've asked him, "Nate, what about when Mommy is really old? Will you love me even then?" He always pats my cheek and smiles. "I'll always love you, Mommy!"

"What about days when I'm cranky? Do you love me even then?"

Nate giggles. "Everyone is cranky sometimes. Of course, I'll love you."

One day, Nate climbed into my lap and sighed, "Hey, Mom?"

"Yes, buddy?"

"What if I did something really bad? Would you love me even then?"

I smiled and kissed the top of his head, squeezing him close. "Sweetie, it doesn't matter how much you mess up or how many awesome things you do. Nothing will ever, ever keep me from loving you."

"What if I couldn't speak? Would you love me even then?"

A lump rose in my throat. My boy doesn't even remember those early years of frustration—the tears, the worries—but I will never be able to erase them from my memory, because it was then that Jesus showed me perfect love and perfect peace.

Love never fails. And as love perseveres, grace continues to pour out blessings and peace. Indeed, there is nothing stickier than a love that refuses to let go.

When people ask me how Nate is doing, I smile and say, "Just fine." He's thriving. God has seen to it. I'll keep my eyes fixed and my heart melded to Jesus. He is my hope and peace. Fear has no chance against such a love. He has promised never to leave me or forsake me, and He has given that same promise to my little boy.

Nate's story is just beginning.

Prayer for a Peace-Filled Life

Father, thank You for Your perfect love. Remind us to praise You, not only when times are good, but when they seem overwhelming too. I praise You for being the God who commands fear to flee in Your presence. May my heart ever cling to Yours. Amen.

Ask and it will be given to you; seek and you will find; knock and the door will be opened to you.

Luke 11:9 (NIV)

WE ARE BLESSED with a God who cares about our every need and will move heaven and earth to fulfill His will for us. My hairdresser, Claribel, witnessed this firsthand through her fourteen-year-old son, Denzel.

Denzel struggled so much in middle school that Claribel held him back in seventh grade. He was devastated when all of his friends moved ahead and he didn't. But by the grace of God, he saw it as an opportunity to prove himself so it would never happen again. He gave school everything he had and his grades soared because of it.

Finally realizing his own potential, he set his eyes on an elite private high school. As much as Claribel wanted to support him, she knew it wasn't feasible. As a single mother raising two boys on a hairdresser's income, there was no way she could afford the tuition. Denzel wouldn't be swayed. He told Claribel that not only was he going to apply and get in but that he also was going to get one of the few scholarships the school offered. He got the applications for both, filled them out, and asked Claribel to review them before he sent them in. Then he began talking about *when* he'd be accepted for both, not *if*.

Lo and behold, Denzel was accepted and received a scholarship! Beyond proud of him, Claribel told a handful of her closest clients about it. What she didn't share was the news she got after that: The annual fees of $2,600 were not included in the scholarship. Trying to figure out how she could come up with that kind of money kept her awake night after night. Filled with dread, she realized she was going to have to tell Denzel he had to give up the scholarship and all of his dreams.

Then her phone rang. It was the principal of the school calling to say that Linda, one of Claribel's trusted clients, had called him after hearing about the scholarship. She wanted to see what she could do to help. When Linda heard about the $2,600 in fees, she paid it—in full, for all four years!

God meets our needs according to the riches of His glory—His promise that He will provide for all our needs, rewarding us for our faith and trust in Him. God rewarded Claribel and Denzel through the gift of an angel, Linda. In the words of Claribel, "Angels don't just live in heaven; they walk the earth."

While our needs might not be met through the help of an angel, we can be certain that God will meet every need. When we depend on Him for provision, He gives us the strength to be content regardless of our circumstances. Moreover, that contentment comes with deep peace.

—Claire McGarry

Let the peace of Christ rule in your hearts, since as members of one body you were called to peace. And be thankful.

Colossians 3:15 (NIV)

DON'T CHANGE A THING!

By Roberta Messner

IN TWO WEEKS, the ladies' group at my church was scheduled to have their Christmas meeting at my old log cabin. I took a long look at my living room and gave myself a good talking-to. *You're a stylist for all those home decor magazines, Roberta. They'll expect a lot more than this.*

My place was a homey hodgepodge of things I'd picked up here and there—objects from garage sales, flea markets, and estate sales. Even curbside finds on trash day. I was always telling magazine subjects how their every treasure had a story behind it that was more valuable than the item. That it was the uniqueness of these objects that made us choose their place to feature.

But with my church get-together coming up, I saw my own belongings with new eyes. Those time-softened quilts and chairs I'd recovered with retro yardage simply would not do. Folks were coming who had never been to my home. Folks I had to impress.

• • •

I'd moved to the century-old West Virginia log cabin over two decades before, after my divorce. It had needed a ton of work, but it spoke to me of a new beginning. When a worker suggested I set a match to it, I paid him no mind. The ramshackle place was falling-down perfect in my book. I took a crowbar to warped walls and discovered original glistening chestnut logs. I refinished the heart-pine floors and added color with touches of wallpaper and paint.

Suddenly that wasn't enough.

Everyone's idea of beauty is different, of course, but back then I was certain: If God lavishes his world with extravagant loveliness, the place I called home needed loveliness too. My personal vision of it. If it had heart, I called it art. I enlisted tartan wool blankets the VFW once gave to Veterans. No one else seemed to be noticing them, so I picked them up for pocket change and hung them from wooden pegs in my living room. Every time I looked at them, the stories of my beloved veteran patients returned to me. And I was always reimagining forgotten objects like antique coffee grinders and adorable handcrafted children's cottages into lamps. The simple act of creativity moved my mind and my hands. It became a connection to the Master Creator—a form of prayer, really. Whenever I switched those lamps on, my heart was in tune with Jesus, the Light of the World. I felt glad, more positive and grateful. I even slept better.

I was at peace. Until now.

If I got right on it, I could have that outdated wingback chair reupholstered in the black-and-white ticking I'd spotted at that pricey home goods shop. My claw-foot oak coffee table could be buffed to a soft sheen with that new paste wax. If I replaced those tired dishes in my corner cupboard with the flashier majolica china I'd packed away, the space could take on the French country look everyone had been talking about. I pulled up homes on Pinterest, scoured my shelter magazines for inspiration, and then made a list of some quick changes I could handle.

The only thing that really changed was the level of my discontent.

• • •

As I readied my house for the gathering, one of my editors telephoned. "We're thinking that darling kitchen you found for us should be a cover," she said. "It's so personal. Authentic. Says 'country' like nothing else." I'd discovered the tiny cabin when I made a wrong turn and ended up in a West Virginia holler (known to people in Appalachia as a remote place). Next thing I knew I was at the wood plank door gushing over the place, hoping against hope they'd invite me inside.

The kitchen did not disappoint. Instead of the stock cabinets everyone else has, these folks had created a one-of-a-kind look with a freestanding antique pie safe complete with pierced tins, an old possum-belly cupboard, a vintage Hoosier with a working flour sifter and bread drawer. Below the old porcelain sink rescued from a salvage yard, they'd gathered authentic feed sacks in a prairie rose pattern to create a skirt. The one in the center still had the words "Chicken Feed." The only window treatment was a vintage apron. It looked like a pioneer kitchen of old. I'd never seen anything so perfect in its imperfections.

My editors were over the moon at the preliminary shots. "Absolutely magical," they declared. "Arrange a shoot for this December, Roberta. It hardly needs a thing. We're seeing it with a spindly Charlie Brown tree and a gingerbread garland at the window." I heard a long chuckle on the other end of the phone. "But this is New York talking. You're in West Virginia. Do whatever feels right and you can't go wrong."

I couldn't wait to see Jake and Patsy Willis again. Their place was so far up the holler they'd practically had to pipe in sunshine. When I'd left that day, I'd rolled down my car window for a final chat. Patsy leaned inside and I gave her shoulder a little squeeze. "Now don't change a thing," I told her. "Your home tells your story. There's nothing better than that!"

Jake nodded and smiled. "You really fancy our little shack?" he said, turning to Patsy. His grin brimmed with marvel. "Whattaya know?"

• • •

The day of the shoot couldn't arrive soon enough. Maybe I'd get my mind off the gathering I'd soon be hosting, even pick up a few ideas for my own ramshackle cabin. But when I stepped inside that darling place, I barely recognized the kitchen. Gone were the one-of-the-kind freestanding cupboards. In their place were stock cabinets. They were lovely, but so much for that uniquely wonderful cover story. They'd lost every smidgen of individuality. The camera crew and I were heartsick. "Tell you what," I heard the photographer say. "If we could move a few of those quaint old cupboards back in here, I believe we can make it work. We gotta get your story back."

As the guys hauled them inside from the garage, I realized an authentic look wasn't the only thing that had vanished. Peace had left the premises as well. "You wouldn't believe all the money I spent to do this," I heard Jake groan. "All. That. Overtime. I'm exhausted." Seems Patsy had pulled up Pinterest and decided the darling cupboards they'd found at out-of-the-way shops wouldn't do. Sounded all too familiar.

Back home, I saw my humble place as if for the first time. Thanks to Jake and Patsy, I'd follow my own sage advice and not change a thing to welcome my ladies' group. When they arrived, I would open my heart and home and welcome them. Let my cabin hug them as it does me. Let the Light of the World, the source of that warmth, fill their spirits.

Through the most unexpected of circumstances, my contentment and joy were back in full measure. My perfectly imperfect place of peace was more than enough.

Prayer for a Peace-Filled Life

Prince of Peace, keep me ever focused on You, not on what I think I lack.

Fear not, for I have redeemed you;
I have called you by your name;
You are Mine.

Isaiah 43:1 (NKJV)

NAMED BY GOD

By Kate Rietema

WE STEPPED OFF THE ELEVATOR onto the seventh floor of a large pediatric hospital. Stickers on our winter coats identified me and my husband as visitors.

Machines hummed, monitors beeped, and night nurses slipped in and out of patient rooms. We found room 713, and a staff member introduced us to ten-day-old baby Larry. He looked smaller than I expected. Half his head was shaved and a large incision snaked its way around his skull. Larry was recovering from a skull fracture, torn neck ligaments, and a large subdural hematoma.

The nurse educated me on how to work with his spinal immobilizer, and what was expected for follow-up appointments and therapy. I signed some papers and tucked his tiny brace-clad body into the car seat I had carried in. It was just after midnight when we left down the long, dim hallway that led to the parking lot and a new chapter of life with baby Larry.

• • •

Earlier that day, a caseworker had stopped by our house, asking if we could take Larry. We were brand-new foster parents, and he would be our first placement. Our daughters were young—a three-year-old and a five-month-old—and although we were excited to foster, the request had come sooner than we expected. My husband and I discussed the sparse details we were given, and then we sat down with our three-year-old, Sierra.

"There is a little baby who needs someone to take care of him and love him a whole bunch," I told Sierra. "Do you know anyone who could do that?"

Her face lit up, and with every ounce of preschooler enthusiasm, Sierra said that *she* could do it.

Sierra was sleeping by the time we arrived home with baby Larry, but I'll always remember the glow on her expectant little face when she came traipsing down the stairs that next morning.

• • •

With two babies in the house, Sierra became my big helper. She and I would sit on the couch, side by side, feeding the babies together. She had a hard time remembering Larry's name, so she referred to him as "the cute little baby."

Somehow, the name Larry never seemed to fit him anyway. In fact, one morning I was talking to Larry in that gentle, expression-filled way many people talk to newborns, and I said to him, "I think that one day your name will be Benjamin." I said this somewhere between unzipping his pajamas and grabbing a clean outfit—and I never gave my words another thought.

Dressing Larry was a delicate task. I tried to choose outfits I could slide on without having to remove his brace entirely. That brace and the scar that formed as his incision healed were constant reminders of Larry's trauma and loss. His past was so painful and his future so unknown. My heart throbbed with whys and hows, until I did the only thing I knew to do—I whispered God's promises in Isaiah 43:1–2 (NKJV) over him:

> Fear not, for I have redeemed you; I have called you by your name; you are Mine. When you pass through the waters, I will be with you; and through the rivers, they shall not overflow you. When you walk through the fire, you shall not be burned, nor shall the flame scorch you.

These words reminded me that before Larry was mine or anyone else's, he was God's. No matter what trauma Larry had suffered, he was under the Lord's protection. God had a plan for this baby, and I could trust it.

Those early months felt like a blur. I was full of purpose and enthusiasm for this life I felt called to love, yet I was also exhausted and overwhelmed. I would gawk with envy at the handicapped spaces as I lugged two infant car seats from the far end of the grocery store parking lot. Then once inside, I awkwardly maneuvered the aisles with two grocery carts, because the babies didn't leave enough room for food.

When I got home and the groceries were put away and the babies were fed and changed, I would nestle my three precious children onto my lap and we would read. My arms were so full I could hardly turn the pages—and my heart was full too. It was in these quieter moments that the tide of exhaustion would recede and the waves of worry for Larry's future would wash in.

Over the next few months, appointments with Larry's neurosurgeon and pediatrician confirmed that he was healing well from his physical injuries—but more than just his skull had been fractured.

Broken families don't heal as easily as bones, I thought when we learned that Larry wouldn't be able to return home to his birth parents.

Dear God, who will be his mom? I prayed. *Is it me?*

I went to his court appointments, sat in doctor offices, and did his therapies. I fed him, bathed him, and rocked him to sleep. I kissed his cheeks, tickled his toes, and prayed over him. I loved him. And yet, I didn't feel like I was his mom. It was a hard thing to say out loud. It made me feel guilty. A better person would jump at the chance to love him forever, right? I wanted the very best for Larry, but somehow that didn't feel like it included me. Would we find the perfect family for him? Would he find the place where he belongs?

When his caseworker asked the question—asked if we would like to adopt him—I choked out a tearful "no." A "no" that I knew would lead to a goodbye. And although I didn't feel like I was meant to be his mom, it would hurt to let him go.

After making that official decision, I cried for days.

• • •

A pre-adoptive family was found for Larry, and our agency set up a placement meeting to create a transition plan. Around the conference room table sat a few staff members and caseworkers, as well as Larry's birth mother. There was also Kathleen—the pre-adoptive mother—and myself—the foster mother. We went around the table, each one introducing ourselves and stating what we hoped to discuss at the meeting.

When it was the birth mother's turn, she faced Kathleen and asked, "If you adopt Larry, would you be willing to change his name?"

We were all surprised by her question.

"Yes, we would," answered Kathleen.

"Good," said the birth mother. "Would you consider changing his name to Benjamin?"

"Yes," Kathleen said. "That is the exact name we have already chosen for him."

A memory tumbled into my mind—back to the morning, months earlier, when the name Benjamin slipped from my lips without much of a thought.

In that moment, around that conference room table, all my worries and guilt and exhaustion melted away. The only thing left was peace. God had named this baby. And then He pressed that name into the hearts of each of his three mothers. God saw each one of us, as well as the list of worries we carried. And He met our needs with a name. Benjamin. Before this baby belonged to his birth mother, or to me, or to Kathleen—he belonged to God.

Benjamin was adopted by Kathleen, and over the years I've been able to watch him grow. Surrounded by a loving family, Benjamin's favorite things include swimming, kitten cuddles, and farm animals. Benjamin has some lasting effects from the trauma to his brain, and life is often hard for him, but I see why God, in all His wisdom, chose Kathleen to be his mother. Their trials and their victories are a beautiful reminder that when we submit our struggles to the Lord, we encounter His unfailing strength.

Prayer for a Peace-Filled Life

Dear God, as I step into what You have called me to do, help me to trust that You will meet all my needs. Amen.

But godliness with contentment is great gain. For we brought nothing into the world, and we can take nothing out of it.

1 Timothy 6:6–7 (NIV)

JEALOUSY AND GREED are as old as time. When given permission to take root in our hearts, they grow at an alarming rate, killing off peace as they expand. Soon they dictate our thoughts and actions, tempting us to make wrong choices that lead us down a path that's detrimental to both our heart and soul.

God gives us free will so that we can make our own choices. He did so with Adam and Eve, providing them with a perfect paradise in the Garden of Eden and telling them they could eat from any tree except the Tree of Knowledge. Through manipulation, the snake—the enemy—convinced Eve that she should want more. She gave in to that temptation and her own greed, costing her the opportunity to remain in the Garden with the King of Peace Himself.

We all have snakes of greed and envy in our lives. They slither in while we're scrolling through social media or peering over the fence into our neighbor's yard, comparing ourselves and our lives to others. Succumbing to the notion that what we've already been given just isn't good enough, we end up wanting more—the perfect appearance with the "right" body, house, and clothes, or the important job with prestige, influence, and power. The more we fixate on what we don't have, the more our vision gets skewed.

Shifting our gaze to recognize what we do have radically alters our perspective. Suddenly, we notice all that we've been blessed with. With our new eyes of appreciation, we see past the enemy's temptation to want more, and toward those blessings that could become our own Garden of Eden if we just look at them the right way.

When we maintain a mindset of contentment and gratitude for who we are, what we have, and where we are going based on God's plan for us, we embrace a godliness that leads to great gain.

—Claire McGarry

The steps of a man are established by the LORD, when he delights in his way; though he fall, he shall not be cast headlong, for the LORD upholds his hand.

Psalm 37:23–24 (ESV)

LOVE STORY

By Elsa Kok Colopy

THEY SAY YOU FIND LOVE when you're not looking. Truth be told, I wasn't very good at not looking. I tried. I ignored good-looking men. I looked the other way or feigned busyness when they walked on by. But the reality was, I was still glancing out of the corner of my eyes. I noticed. As a single mom for twelve years, I longed for the companionship of a wonderful guy. I was willing to wait on our God, but the longing (and the looking) remained.

It was worse earlier on. I had started my single-parent journey unwilling to wait on God at all. I got into some unhealthy relationships that wounded both my daughter and me. At the end of one more heartbreak, I couldn't stand it any longer. I needed Jesus. After a long hiatus from church, I darkened the doors of an old Methodist church in Indiana. The congregation was older and happy to see a young soul come into their community. Even when I tried to sneak out right after service, they surrounded me, cornering me with their love. And they showed me Jesus. They modeled His kindness, they exuded His joy, and they were authentic in their deep faith.

Even though I was broken in many ways, they invited me into their homes and made me feel welcome. I wanted what they had. So I asked, and they shared. They discipled me and taught me about God's love and character; I grew by leaps and bounds. Jesus now came first and in the dating world, that meant my choices were much slimmer. It was truly tough to find a man who loved God and loved people well.

• • •

So when I went to speak at a conference in Arizona on single-parent ministry, I was looking but not looking. I had a book table set up there, and a handsome guy stopped by for a chat. I admit I looked. Maybe twice. Throughout the conference, he stopped by several more times, and I found myself looking for him in breaks between seminars. He was engaging, kind, and a good conversationalist. It seemed like we had quite a bit in common. He was a single dad; I was a single mom. He was active in ministry; I was too. We both loved the outdoors and seemed to roll with the punches when it came to life stressors.

When I left the conference, Brian promised to stay in touch. I looked forward to it. But then life got busy. Two months later, I received an email, "I don't know if you remember me, but..."

Oh yes, I remembered!

We began an email conversation and over the next several months talked through the hard questions. We shared the good pieces of our story, but also talked through the heartaches and the failures. We wanted to be as honest as we could to see if there might be hope for a future.

Our relationship progressed, but I found myself nervous about making another mistake. I knew I had to invite people into the process. If the people closest to me saw red flags, I would choose to listen—unlike other times in my life. As the youngest of five with four older brothers, I thought it would be good to introduce Brian to my big brothers as well. They loved me, knew me, and would give me a clear picture of whether this guy was the real deal.

Brian was a trooper, willing to sit through the hard questions and glaring looks. It was even more fun when Brian put me through the same paces. He had a mentor in his life who had seen him go through a devastating divorce. This man was deeply protective of Brian's faith journey and laid out a tract on exactly what it looked like to accept Jesus into my heart. I was happy to tell him that Jesus had resided there for a good long while and was actually an excellent housekeeper. He'd cleared out a lot. Brian's mentor smiled but still dug in to make sure I wasn't just making myself look the role of Christian lady.

With green lights all around, our relationship continued to move forward. I prayed incessantly about it—fighting the nervousness of a lifetime of bad decisions. I only wanted this relationship if it was truly of God. Could Brian truly be the one for me?

• • •

When Brian asked me to marry him, I'd had a sneaky suspicion it was coming. He was nervous when he invited me to a fancy restaurant, and he was never nervous. I was nervous when I accepted his dinner invitation. I remember changing outfits in the closet of my home, my daughter with me. We had the whole house to ourselves, but somehow were jammed into the closet with the door shut as she held up different outfits to my shoulders. This one. No, this. We finally settled on a simple black dress. I promised to call her the minute anything happened. "I really like this guy, Mom."

"Me, too, sweetheart."

We arrived at the restaurant. It was the type of place where they pull out your chair and then place the napkin on your lap for you. Super fancy. Before we ordered, I saw the waitress come over with a bottle of champagne in hand. "Congratulations!" She said, smiling big. I could almost feel Brian to the side of me, motioning that now was not the time. He hadn't even asked yet! I played dumb and smiled like I had no idea what she was talking about. She fumbled, hemmed, and hawed before continuing, "Congratulations . . . on your night out!"

"Awwww," I said. "How sweet!"

Brian sighed in relief. I continued to gush, "How nice that they celebrate our night out like that!"

We enjoyed a spectacular meal of small portions at outrageous prices and chatted away. The nerves eased as we fell into our joyful connection of conversation and laughter. After the plates were cleared, he invited me outside to a walking bridge that overlooked a beautiful lake. It was prom night, so there were multiple high schoolers crossing over and laughing loudly. He took a few deep breaths and waited for a break in the traffic. He got down on one knee and professed his love. He told me all the things he loved about me and then pulled out the ring. "Will you marry me?"

"Yes, oh yes!" He slipped the ring on my finger and stood. He took me in his arms and planted a gentle kiss. Together we turned to look out over the water. There, as only God can do, floated two swans. Their beaks leaned close together and their necks were shaped into a perfect heart.

I gasped. "Get out! Did you hire them?"

He laughed. I laughed. We continued to watch the swans nuzzle in their shape of a heart, and we felt God's pleasure on a relationship He had ordained, orchestrated, and delighted in. His peace flooded our hearts, His joy our marriage.

Seventeen years later, He is still smiling.

And so are we.

Prayer for a Peace-Filled Life

Oh Lord, You are my peace. Thank You for leading me and directing my steps. Even when I take risks, if You are leading the way, I can live at peace. Help me to always lean into Your direction and hold on to Your peace.

And we know that in all things God works for the good of those who love him, who have been called according to his purpose.

Romans 8:28 (NIV)

MY MOST PEACEFUL NIGHT'S SLEEP

By Ben Cooper

I WAS IN A HOSPITAL GOWN waiting my turn for an MRI. I was sent there the day before by my ENT physician for a CT scan to figure out what was going on with my sinuses. A younger man sat near me nervously shaking his legs. I asked him if he was OK. "No! I am claustrophobic and am afraid to go into the tube." I encouraged him to take the earplugs they offer to help reduce the relentless hammering noise the machine makes. I commented, "I am more afraid of the results than the machine."

They handed me the MRI results and I hand-delivered them to my doctor's office. The doctor studied the images and asked if he could take a biopsy right then; it's normally done as outpatient same-day surgery, but a sense of urgency abounded. Of course, I said yes. Wow! That was painful—having a biopsy taken from my upper sinus passage without a sedative. He said to expect a call when the results came back.

A week later, the phone rang. My doctor said, "You have cancer." His proclamation shocked me and made it impossible to process any of his other words except to call his office in the morning. I hung up the phone and found it difficult to share the diagnosis with my wife, Sonia.

• • •

Sinus cancer, seriously? I have never smoked a cigarette in my life. We just had our fifth child at the end of the previous year and I thought I was in good health. This wasn't supposed to happen. How bad was it? Did I just get handed a death sentence? Peace of any kind eluded us as we tried to process the limited information and what to do.

When I called the doctor the next morning, he had already scheduled an appointment with an ENT oncologist in Baltimore. Sonia and I began requesting prayers from our family, friends, and church. I never asked God, "Why me? Why now?" Things were happening so quickly that it was all we could do to keep up with appointments, tests, and procedures.

This was the first of many trips we would make to Baltimore, three hours each way. The oncologist confirmed the diagnosis as an aggressive adenocarcinoma and scheduled an appointment with a neurosurgeon. Sonia and

I weren't prepared for the extensive explanation of the invasive procedure nor the 35-percent survival rate of this kind of cancer.

The hectic weeks leading up to surgery included times of prayer for guidance and strength. I had a ton of medical paperwork to complete, including updating our will to give Sonia medical power of attorney and writing an advance directive. I also filed for the Family Medical Leave Act to protect my job. I had plenty of questions but continued praying. Peace seemed elusive due to the rapid pace of everything happening, but my trust in the Lord never wavered. I knew I had a growing concert of prayers reaching God's throne room on my behalf.

I struggled to find quality time with my family, and work was always demanding in the spring. Our newborn was three months old, and we decided to have a church dedication the day before my surgery. It would be a time to focus on family, our calm before the storm. My brother would make the two-hour drive with my parents from north of Pittsburgh and we would head to Baltimore in the afternoon. We told our four older children, all under the age of ten, that I had to go away from home to have an operation. They would be cared for by a family member and Sonia would bring our newborn. Our plans were all set.

• • •

Five days before the dedication, we received a phone call from the hospital telling Sonia I was scheduled for a stealth MRI the day before we were planning to leave. This specialized MRI was vital for surgery because it would map out the position of the cancer so the doctors could accurately navigate the instruments. But that not-so-little change crumbled our plans. In tears, Sonia called me at work to relay the message, knowing the baby dedication would have to be canceled. I echoed the frustration and disappointment in her voice. How dare they!

I called the hospital and adamantly shared my concern about leaving out this vital piece of information. They'd managed to destroy the only ray of sunshine we'd had over the last few weeks. And this change not only affected me but also my wife, our five children, my parents, my brother, and my church. I had been trying to reduce my stress prior to surgery, and this only added to it. That phone call devastated our plans and stripped away what little control—and peace—I had.

My final week was filled with pressure—wrapping up work, dealing with last-minute medical paperwork, postponing the baby's dedication, and thinking about my family and that survival rate. I felt like I was in a room where the ceiling and walls were squeezing in. Then God's still, small voice reassured me He was in control. Quietly through the chaos, little glimpses of God began surfacing.

I agreed to find a place for my family to stay in Baltimore for the first three days after surgery. I needed an extra room attached for Sonia and the baby. I finally found one that met our needs, but it was expensive. A work friend called to see how I was doing and asked if I needed a place for my family to stay, and I told him I'd just reserved a room. He told me his daughter worked for a hotel chain and offered to make the reservations using her employee discount. It turns out she worked for the same hotel chain I had just booked. Her discount lowered the cost by a hundred dollars per day. God used a friend to do that.

We spent the night before surgery with a Christian family I've known for years. They graciously opened their home and invited their adult children to come to pray. They anointed my head with frankincense, removing another layer of stress and reminding me of God's peace and protection.

I thought it would be hard getting a good night's rest while facing life-threatening cancer, exploratory surgery, and survival odds not in my favor. Yet, I experienced my most peaceful night's sleep ever. I rose early with nothing to worry about.

I had asked another friend to drive us to the hospital to relieve the stress of dealing with Baltimore traffic. My brother and parents met us in the surgical waiting room. Our pastor and his wife were there too. Although the past month hadn't gone quite as I had planned, God brought me to this moment surrounded by family and friends.

I was prepped for surgery with my support team there. The lead surgeon explained the procedure and told how the family could be kept updated on my progress. As our pastor laid his hands on me and began to pray, I felt another set of hands touching me. I looked up and saw they were the hands of my surgeon. Complete peace overwhelmed me that can only come from God. He was letting me know that He truly was in control of everything.

• • •

The surgery lasted ten and a half hours. I was in the ICU for a week and lost three days due to being heavily sedated. Following surgery and a short recovery period at home, I stayed six and a half weeks in Baltimore undergoing 130 radiation treatments and spent each weekend resting at home. I was out of work for a total of five months. Looking back, I know God was in control all the time.

Stress and chaos aren't easy to deal with, but God taught me a lesson during that difficult time in my life when He gave me my most peaceful night's sleep ever: He puts people in our lives who are "called according to His purpose."

Prayer for a Peace-Filled Life

Father God, guide me in remembering that only You can provide perfect peace. Grant me the peace that allowed Jesus to be asleep in the boat while the storm raged. Give me peaceful rest when I need it most. Amen.

And my God will meet all your needs according to the riches of his glory in Christ Jesus.

Philippians 4:19 (NIV)

PEACE LIKE A RAGING RIVER

By Sarah Greek

THE CHEMICAL IMBALANCES in my brain tell me often and very loudly that I want to die. Though I know deeply in my soul I do not want that at all, the emotional and mental pain can be excruciating and all-consuming. Since my mortal brain and body is not designed to carry that kind of turmoil on a constant basis, my self-preservation mechanism will activate and flood me with thoughts of escape rather than harm.

Sometimes those thoughts are constant and without reprieve, unless I interrupt them with a very fragile dance of strong prayer, powerful meds, an empathetic therapist, and an arsenal of coping skills. Easier said than done most days.

One of my best coping strategies is going for a hike, preferably somewhere by water. That space in nature, the movement of water, and lack of artificial stimuli combine to lull my oversaturated system into a less fractured state. I can breathe, and I can think a complete thought for a minute or two, maybe even in full color instead of the standard gray of depression. Some days, a simple walk in the woods can be a literal lifesaver.

• • •

Late one winter, we experienced two straight weeks of combined weather that kept us pretty much locked up inside. A big dump of snow came down fast and heavy, and then turned to ice so we couldn't even play in it. It then turned to drenching rain. Due to the warmer temps, the piles of ice and snow just dissolved into gray-brown slush, and we all sank into muddy despair. I was climbing the walls, the kids following suit. My husband finally had enough and sent me out on my own for a hike. I chose my favorite trail with a waterfall; I imagined the falls would be roaring with all the recent precipitation.

The trailhead starts at the base of several drops of waterfalls wandering down the side of the mountain. After turning sharply up a series of switchbacks, the trail crosses the ridge of the mountain and the river below before descending down into a section of quiet woods and back out to the start. Sometimes we'd see eagles from the lookout points over the river. Sometimes the boys had found salamanders, and various times of the year offered a wide array of variegated mushrooms in hues almost fantastical.

I was relieved this day to find that the dirt road to the trailhead was open and passable. I wasn't sure how much flooding the river would have experienced with these recent storms, and as I parked just down from the dam, I could hear the din of the water before I even shut the engine off. I took a quick peek before I started out and noted the river was not quite flooded, but it was definitely angry, churning, and rushing toward less saturated shores. The power of water is truly humbling.

I turned and started up the trail, praying to be knit back together by nature's sensory massage. But my agitation was long accumulated, my anger hot and prickling. I was so sick of feeling *everything* bad and seemingly *nothing* good. God's Word promises that if I am justified by faith, I would then be granted peace beyond all understanding that would guard my heart and my mind. However, I didn't *feel* guarded or protected and almost never had I felt at peace. And right about then I was feeling pretty salty about it!

Barely registering the beautiful gushing falls, the dripping trees, and freshly scrubbed trail, I pushed up the switchbacks until the boggy air burned in my chest and the incline stretched my calves into burnt rubber. The first lookout provided a good view of the front side of the flooding dam, the water crashing over and pounding the rocks below like thunder. Mentally, I railed over the racket from the river, petitioning God for this elusive "peace," practically demanding to know why I always had to feel like those rocks—buffeted, pummeled, drowned in a roar. Nothing caught under that flow would have a hope of resurfacing. It would be churned into oblivion and join the riverbed as dust. "Why am I *always* there!" I cried. "And where in the world are *You* while I feel like I'm drowning?" All I heard was nature's silence.

The ridge trail wandered serpentinely along the crest, taking me from river lookouts to deeper forest avenues that smelled rich with wet earth and decaying wood and back again to another view. The miles melted away but the heaviness seemed to cling.

The final leg before the descent opened to a view of the dam downstream a ways, a stretch of river proceeding it now visible. There, stretched across the river, was a string of orange buoys, behind which lay a chaos of debris, including entire fallen trees and large unidentifiable objects submerged to unknown depths. The mass covered a solid 50 feet or more of the oncoming river, straining against the line that allowed only water to continue down and over the damn. Without those strong buoys in place, I imagined the damage that debris would cause—clogging the river's flow as they dropped over the dam in an unmovable tangle, maybe even splitting the rocks below as they made impact, completely altering the trajectory of this water.

• • •

My breath caught as God spoke: "I am *there*. My peace promises I will never let pass that which would damage you." I drifted my gaze again to the rocks below, deluged with water cleared of debris. My heart breaking, I asked,

"But why can't You catch me too? Why do I have to tumble and fall?"

"Because you don't belong back there in the broken mess. I will always sweep you clear, so your journey can continue in freedom and safety. The base of the falls is always loud and torrential, but it is also never, ever stagnant. You can rest there and know it is a renewed well every single second."

The walk back to my car was contemplative, with a significant lack of weightiness at last. That image of a strong line of buoys holding back the mass from the free flow of the dam has lived in my mind ever since that hike, and I draw it up whenever feelings of being unprotected and turbulent swell in me. He is right *there.*

Prayer for a Peace-Filled Life

Thank You for protecting me and holding me in perfect peace even when I feel the torrential storms of life. Thank You for hearing my small cries and railing roars. And thank You for a natural world full of pictures that tell Your truths. Amen.

The LORD will fight for you; you need only to be still.

Exodus 14:14 (NIV)

AN UNEXPECTED ANSWER TO PRAYER

By Terri J. Kirby

EVEN AT AN EARLY AGE, our minds begin to form ideas about what our futures will hold for us. Dreams are shaped by our circumstances and the people around us. Raised in a loving home with an amazing extended family, including numerous aunts fostered by my grandparents, my deepest desire as I grew into early adulthood was to marry, have children, and raise a family.

Although not related to me legally or by blood, I consider these women my "aunts" and always will. So many fond memories of my childhood with them flood my mind—piggyback rides, carrying me everywhere, playing games with me. As a petite child with dwarfism who time spent in the hospital and at home recuperating in a body cast, I was showered with love and attention from family and friends. Growing up, it was a given in my mind that I would one day have a large family of my own, with a slew of children to love and care for as I had been.

• • •

Thirty-some years ago, as I was desperately desiring to become a mom, my dreams of giving birth were thwarted when my husband and I decided the numerous surgeries I'd had for my disability made it impractical and unsafe for me to carry a child. I feel blessed to have had an amazing surgeon who loved little people and was sought by parents of little people from around the world. I underwent numerous hip, leg, and ankle surgeries throughout my childhood and my teen years, and I believe I would not be walking today if it were not for Dr. Kopits and his expertise.

After deciding it was too risky to put the weight of a baby on my fragile frame, I was devastated and struggled to come to terms with my new reality of not expanding our family. My heart broke as I watched family and friends welcoming children into their homes, knowing that my husband and I would not. Sure, I was happy for them, but I asked God why I couldn't have a child of my own too. I was certain I would be a good mom, giving them as much love, if not more, than any other mom. I had such a love for children, and I experienced more and more pain as I continued to work with them through Sunday school and Bible school.

The hurt became so unbearable that I began to stay home on Mother's Day. It was simply too painful to see all of the happy moms with their little ones. Other days, my heart would sink as I saw parents smiling with their giggly children, feeling as though I was being punched in the stomach at the sight and sounds of a happy family talking and laughing together. That seems so selfish to me now to say that outright, but I'll admit it was true.

One night, the pain was so overwhelming that I cried myself to sleep—and not for the first time. On that particular night, I was at the end of my strength, and I cried out to God, begging Him to help me accept His will in this situation, to help me handle it emotionally and move on. I drifted off to sleep as tears soaked my pillow.

That night, I had a very vivid dream. I dreamed that I actually, physically gave birth and went through the feelings and emotions of childbirth. When I awoke, I knew it was a dream, but it seemed so realistic. It's odd that I didn't wake up feeling disappointed and even more depressed that it wasn't true. Instead, I had an unusual peace. Somehow, I was no longer distraught about not being able to have a child. A deep contentment and satisfaction washed over me. I could carry on. I could accept not being a mom.

• • •

Fast-forward a few years, and my husband and I were on our way home from a Little People of America camping weekend. We both had a wonderful weekend with our friends (as usual), and we both had enjoyed spending time with the average-sized parents and their children with dwarfism. On that trip home, my husband suggested that perhaps we should consider adoption. I hadn't thought he would be open to the idea, because neither of us knew much about it. But that's all it took to get me investigating. If he had any second thoughts, it was too late! He had spoken the idea.

Immediately, I searched the Internet for adoption agencies and copied and pasted a form email, stating that we were a little-person couple interested in adopting a little-person child, and asking if they knew of any available children with dwarfism. We received about a dozen responses regarding children within and outside the United States.

As soon as we learned of the little girl named Dasha, who was in a baby home in Russia, we knew she was the one God had intended for us. She was almost four years old, and what a cutie!

I still remember those first days of that first visit in Russia with the little chatterbox who spoke fluent Russian with anyone who would listen. My husband and I learned a little Russian to converse with her and the others we met, but it was minimal. We didn't know what she was discussing with her fellow Russians, but we were sure at least part of it was something along the lines of "Who are these crazy people, and why are they speaking such gibberish?"

We met her in August, then went back for court hearings and to bring her home in October. As a requirement for adoption, during our second trip to Russia, we were finally able to take her to our hotel with us. The bonding was a little challenging (she cried once to go home with our sweet, young Russian interpreter) but mostly it was magical.

In my mind, I can picture like it was yesterday the time we lay on the bed in the hotel as I tried to get her to take a nap. I pretended I was sleeping. Soon I felt a tiny finger touching my eyelids, then my eyelashes, and I knew she was beginning to warm up to me. My heart melted.

Several hours-long surgeries later in her early and teen years, that precious little girl is now an outgoing, smart, funny, and talented young woman, pursuing her master's degree and living life to the fullest. I can't imagine how different our lives would have been without her.

I am amazed and in awe that God, in His wisdom and loving-kindness, knew there was a little girl halfway around the world who needed parents as much as we needed a child. He answered my lifelong prayer to become a mom. But first, He gave me the peace to make it through the waiting period, having no idea what was in store. God can do amazing things for and through us and give us peace in the process.

Prayer for a Peace-Filled Life

Lord, help me to remember that You are always there for me. Let me never forget that You have blessings in store for me, no matter how heavyhearted I feel.

But we had to celebrate and be glad, because this brother of yours was dead and is alive again; he was lost and is found.

Luke 15:32 (NIV)

WE'RE ALL PRONE to wander—from what's right and from God. Although we have a loving and forgiving Father who is always waiting for our return, it's up to us to do the about-face and make our way back to Him. My cousin John is a perfect example.

Despite being raised in the faith, the pull of bad behavior in his teens had John knee-deep in trouble. The police were always at his door. When he finally went off to college, the stress of fighting with his parents, working to pay his way, and attending classes and doing homework were all too much. He quit, met a girl, and moved across the country with her to California. Things only got worse as John drank, did drugs, and made other choices that led to self-gratification.

When there was a big layoff where he worked, John lost his job, then his girlfriend, and finally, his apartment. Homeless and at rock bottom, he found himself in church asking God, "Why have You abandoned me?" Shortly after, his father tracked him down and sent word that he'd gotten John a good job back home. Despite feeling like a failure, John made his way back to Boston.

When John walked through the door of his family home, his parents broke down in tears of joy, then gathered his siblings together to celebrate. As John apologized for all he'd done, his father hugged him and simply said, "I'm your father. I'll always love you."

The unconditional love and forgiveness from his earthly father healed a lot of John's wounds, but they didn't change his ways. It was his future wife, Maria, who did. When she refused to date him because of the drinking and drug use, John quit cold turkey and began reading the Bible she gave him. When John finally asked the Holy Spirit to come into his life, he says the result felt like "a cleansing fire from God's throne burning away his sins and filling him with an inexplicable love."

John's encounter with the unconditional love and forgiveness of his Heavenly Father set the course for his new life. He now devours Scripture as if it's food, volunteers for everything at his church, and loves to share about all the mistakes he's made so he can testify about all the miraculous things God has done for him.

At one time or another we have all experienced some darkness in our heart. Yet it is by God's grace we have been saved (Ephesians 2:8), and for that, we can all celebrate and be glad.

—Claire McGarry

Forget the former things; do not dwell on the past. See, I am doing a new thing! Now it springs up; do you not perceive it? I am making a way in the wilderness and streams in the wasteland.

Isaiah 43:18–19 (NIV)

ARRANGED BY GOD

By Mindy Baker

AS OUR PLANE zipped along at 500 miles per hour, my mind raced even faster. What would happen when we landed in the Czech Republic? Had I made the right choice in agreeing to take this trip?

The events of the past five years had taken their toll. An ugly church split, the betrayal of close friendships, a recent job transition to a new ministry for my husband, and back to work full-time in the classroom for me were just a few of my external issues. But the main problem underlying it all was my hard heart. Bitterness, woundedness, and pretending that I was OK when I so obviously wasn't were the internal battles that had me emotionally crippled and spiritually defeated. Was this trip a mistake?

• • •

Before the trip, I remember writing a specific promise of Scripture on an index card that I kept on my desk in my classroom. Reading these verses from Isaiah 43:18–19 (NIV) always calmed my spirit: "Forget the former things; do not dwell on the past. See, I am doing a new thing! Now it springs up; do you not perceive it? I am making a way in the wilderness and streams in the wasteland." Although I often prayed about my situation, there seemed to be no answer to my pleas and no change in my circumstance.

My husband, Doug, had suggested counseling multiple times, but I kept denying that I needed it, and I refused to pursue it. But deep down, I knew he was right. I *needed* counseling. I just *didn't want* counseling. But God had other plans.

First, my husband's business partner suggested we take a trip to Prague. A friend of his had a ministry there that he wanted us to connect with and learn from. They were using some innovative strategies that he felt we could implement in our own ministry. After we met with them, we would have a few days in Prague to relax and explore the city. "A donor has generously provided the needed funds for most of the trip," he said.

I love to travel, so that was an easy decision! *Of course, I wanted to do that!* However, once I agreed wholeheartedly to go, his next suggestion got more personal. "I know how you have been struggling, Mindy," he said. "My friend's wife has helped hundreds of women, and she is willing to meet with you for counseling if you are open to it."

I got very quiet. In my mind I was thinking, *Nooooooo! I don't want to!* My eyes filled with tears. God's voice seemed to whisper in my ear, *I have arranged this for you, My child. Trust Me.*

"I'll think about it," I said. But in the end, I agreed to go. Even though I was afraid, I went back to the promise that I was claiming on the index card that still sat on my desk at work. Whenever I read it, I would feel a measure of peace in its promise.

• • •

Now, with the roar of the airplane engine filling my ears, it all felt surreal. *What was I doing on this plane? Why had I agreed to travel across the world to pour my heart out to a complete stranger?* My anxious thoughts spun out of control as we drew closer to our destination.

We arrived in Prague, rented a car, set the GPS, and set out for our destination. Navigating the traffic patterns in a country where you can't read or speak the language provided an adventurous cross-cultural experience. We laughed when we saw what we'd ordered for lunch. A few hours later, we finally arrived safely to our hotel, a ski chalet tucked into the side of a scenic mountain. It was during the summer so there was no snow, and the vistas were breathtaking. That night on the patio sitting under the stars, I prayed, asking God for peace and comfort. *I'm scared of this experience; please help me.*

The next morning, two women met with me to talk. They explained that they liked to counsel people in pairs. We awkwardly sat down together, and one of the women said, "Let me pray for our time."

After the prayer, the other women looked up and strangely said, "I sense that God is roaring over you."

"What do you mean?" I asked, as I honestly didn't hear anything. "God is very silent in my life lately," I admitted.

"Well, in the silence, God's presence is roaring over you!" the woman responded.

I wondered what that meant, but even though I didn't know, I felt strangely safe and calm. Her words gave me the peace and courage to share my story. I thought, *I've come all this way. It's now or never.*

I told them about my pain and all the hurt I had been storing up inside. Emotionally speaking, I was deeply wounded. The women listened and walked me through healing tears, but also prayers of both forgiveness and confession. As they listened, together we made a list of specific lies that I had been believing about myself and my experiences. For each lie, God's Word had an answer, and together we found specific scriptures that could counter the lies that clouded my mind.

That day, as I listened for God's gentle whisper, I heard Him telling me specific steps of obedience for me to follow. We wrote those steps down.

- *Set your heart and mind on things above, not on earthly things.*
- *Put to death whatever belongs to the earthly nature.*
- *Believe that God wants your good, not your harm.*
- *Remember that Christ is enough.*
- *Be the Lord's willing servant.*
- *Make your camp in the impossible place.*

During the experience, there was one moment I will never forget—a moment when God brought peace into my heart and revealed His tender loving care to me in a personal way. During our second day together, one of the women who was counseling me said, "Last night, God gave me two verses for you, and I have been waiting for the right time to share them. I think this is the time." She opened her Bible and said emphatically, "God wants you to know that He is doing something new." My eyes grew wide as she read several verses from the book of Isaiah. My lips trembled and the tears began to stream down my face. "Why are you crying?" she asked.

"Those are my verses," I said. "I have had those exact verses written on an index card on my desk at school for the last two years, and I have been praying that God would do a new thing in my heart and in my life."

"I think He's trying to tell you something," she said.

I sat in stunned silence. Had I really traveled halfway around the world to the tiny village of Malenovice, Czech Republic, only to meet two strangers who would listen, counsel with me, pray with me, and then tell me the exact scriptures God had been using to bring peace into my life back home? Was this a coincidence? It couldn't be! God was showing me that He had been making a way in my wilderness all along. He was providing streams in my wasteland to help me heal! He was doing a new thing! And now, I was starting to perceive it!

Prayer for a Peace-Filled Life

Dear God, please fill my heart with peace. Help me to trust that You are doing a new thing in my life even when the circumstances are different than what I would choose.

There is a time for everything, and a season for every activity under the heavens.

Ecclesiastes 3:1 (NIV)

WHEN THE ANSWER IS "NO"

By Norma Poore

HAVE YOU EVER PRAYED needing a specific answer?

Like many people around the world, I like to begin a new year with a game plan. A couple of years ago was no different. I asked God if He would open the door for me to attend the Blue Ridge Mountains Christian Writers Conference and the North Carolina Writers' Network intensive conference. Both of these conferences were only an hour or two from my home.

I prayed for several days but heard nothing. Now what? Experience has taught me to be still whenever I don't have a clear answer from God. I continued to pray and wait for Him to answer. After a few weeks of praying and still no open door or peace about the conferences, I knew the answer: "No."

"But God, You know how much I enjoy conferences," I prayed again. "I get my extrovert fix, which is important since I live with two introverts. Please reconsider?"

God didn't change His mind.

• • •

One morning, a couple of weeks after coming to terms with God's answer, I was in the bathroom and noticed my husband's watch on the counter. Very strange. He rarely forgets it. I opened the bathroom door and looked at the bed. He was still there.

"David. Wake up." I said.

Whoosh sounds came from his mouth.

"Honey. What's wrong?" I asked louder, trying not to panic.

"S. St. St…k," he said as he dropped his head back to the pillow.

"We're going to the hospital," I said.

David got out of bed and dressed himself, but I saw that the right side of his body sagged and he had a harder time making his right arm and leg move. Thankfully, the hospital was a just an eight-minute drive, which I made in five.

"I ordered a CT scan to see where the stroke occurred," the doctor said as he exited our room.

Immediately, I was on my phone calling the family and our pastor. While I texted friends and prayer warriors, God's peace covered me, like the warm blanket covering David. I knew He was with us.

"Matthew, you didn't need to come," I said to our son. "Dad's doing better. We're waiting for the results of a CT scan. The good news is his blood pressure is coming down from 210 over 99."

Matthew hugged his dad and tried unsuccessfully not to cry.

While our son was in the room, I took a few minutes to step away. I prayed, thanking God for His faithfulness, protection, and that David's stroke was mild. The outcome could have been a lot worse. I cried. Once I calmed down, I called my mom and asked her to add David to her church's prayer list, and I promised to keep her updated.

After Matthew left, David was admitted for observation. While we waited on paperwork, two of our pastors popped in for a visit.

"You know, David, if you didn't want to go on the couples retreat this weekend, all you had to do was say so. You didn't have to go to this extreme to get out of it," Pastor C. J. said with a chuckle.

Their presence lightened our moods and they reminded us that God is always in control. I relaxed as fear and worry lessened. I thought of the words in Isaiah 41:10, one of my favorite verses, where God tells us not to fear or be anxious, for He has us in His righteous right hand. I knew God had a plan and purpose for all of this.

• • •

A short time later, the doctor came back into David's room. "Mr. Poore, the scan with contrast shows you did, in fact, have a stroke. We're going to treat it with blood thinners and blood pressure and cholesterol medications. We want to make sure you're on the right medications before you leave. I'm ordering physical and occupational therapy for you, as well. Any questions?"

"No. Thank you, doctor, for explaining this in terms we can understand," I said.

"Take care." And with that, the doctor was gone.

When the therapists came, I watched carefully and took notes on how they did things, so I could duplicate their methods once we were home.

Again, I prayed, thanking God for His faithfulness and asked what we were to learn from this experience. It was difficult watching my husband, who's always been strong and independent, struggle to eat or drink because his mouth didn't work like it's supposed to. I did my best to reassure him.

My husband was protected by God for sure, based on the level of concern that registered on the doctors' faces. But after two-and-a-half days in the hospital, the doctors were pleased with his progress and discharged him with instructions to follow up with our primary doctor.

• • •

Three weeks later, the United States, as well as most of the world, shut down due to COVID-19. During this time, I took David to the ER because he appeared to have had a seizure. The hospital allowed me in the exam room so I could tell the nurse and doctor what happened. Then I was told to leave.

"Are you kidding? I'm not leaving him."

"You have to or I'll call security to escort you out," the nurse said coldly.

"This is wrong. What is wrong with you people? What if he needs me?"

"Norma, just go wait outside. I'll be fine. Go on," David said in his usual calm voice.

I leaned over, kissed him, and said, "Don't you dare die on me." With that I left. I almost ran into the entrance door because the hospital had disabled the mechanism for the doors to open automatically so people couldn't sneak in. I flung the two doors so hard they slammed against the frame, bounced back, and almost closed me between them. My anger was like none I'd felt in a very long time.

"Why, God? You know this is wrong. I need to be in there with him. Please?" Tears burned my eyes. Who could I call at midnight during a tornado watch? I tried calling Mom, but she didn't answer. She was probably sound asleep and didn't hear the phone. I called my best friend. She answered. I told her what happened and she drove twenty minutes to come and sit with me. My van was swaying as strong winds blew around us. God sent her to be His force of calm in my storm, and I'll always be thankful to God and her for being with me.

I'd like to say God healed David and our life returned to normal, but that's not what happened. We made several trips to the doctor in attempts to level out his medications.

But my husband was on too much blood thinner, which caused blood in his urine, so the doctor referred him to a urologist.

The urologist ordered a CT scan of David's abdominal region to get a good look at his kidneys and urinary tract. The results of this test showed innumerable lesions on his pelvic bones, leading to a visit with an oncologist. Once again, I called on our pastors and prayer warriors to intercede on my husband's behalf.

The oncologist asked if we'd seen the scan, to which we replied we hadn't. I followed him to see what the doctor meant by innumerable lesions. And there on David's hips were so many white dots that I stopped counting after I'd reached fifty.

"Doctor, is this cancer?" I asked.

"I've learned not to answer that question. Many times, what appeared to be cancer wasn't," the doctor said.

"So, you've seen God do miracles?"

"Indeed I have."

• • •

David and I spent the rest of the day on the oncology floor of the hospital an hour from home. When all the tests were finished, including a bone biopsy (super painful), we went home and waited for the results.

The middle of the following week, a call came from the oncologist. All David's tests were negative. The doctor had run over twenty different tests and not one showed cancer.

God had heard the prayers offered from all around the world on my husband's behalf and healed him. I also believe that David had a stoke so he'd end up on medicine that resulted in problems requiring a CT scan of his abdomen. And, of course, the "no" I received from God meant that I would be where I was supposed to be according to His plan.

Prayer for a Peace-Filled Life

Father, when I am afraid, remind me of Your great miracles. Help me remember that You orchestrate things for reasons we can't see or understand in the moment. Thank You for not only Your healing power, but also for the grace, peace, and comfort You bestow on us. I never want to forget. I pray in Jesus's name. Amen.

The Lord himself goes before you and will be with you; he will never leave you nor forsake you. Do not be afraid; do not be discouraged.

Deuteronomy 31:8 (NIV)

GUIDING ME HOME

By Jennie Ivey

MY HANDS WERE white-knuckled on the steering wheel. At least I assumed they were. In the dark of night, I could hardly see my hands or anything else except never-ending headlights and taillights moving at breakneck speed as I headed east on Interstate 40.

The only thought running through my head was that I must have been crazy to have said yes when a friend invited me to this evening's performance of the Nashville Symphony. I'd reached the age when I was nervous about driving on busy highways, even in the daytime. I absolutely despised driving in the dark. Add to that a 90-mile journey home once the concert was over and it was no wonder I was feeling panicky.

• • •

The friend who'd asked me to join him lived in Nashville but had never been to the symphony. He'd been gifted box seats with a bird's-eye view of the orchestra and, knowing that I'd never been to the symphony either, wanted to share his good fortune with me. That in itself was reason enough to accept, but what really tipped the scales was that the performance was on Holy Saturday, the day before Easter. The program? Handel's *Messiah*. Who could say no to such an invitation, despite the long drive?

We enjoyed a lovely dinner before making our way to the symphony hall and finding our seats. It wasn't long before chorus and orchestra members began tuning up. Then the lights went down and the audience was swept into the story of the birth, life, death, and resurrection of Jesus Christ. I'd always thought of Handel's *Messiah* as a fixture of the Christmas season because my church choir performed portions of it, including the Hallelujah Chorus, every December. But as I studied the history of *Messiah* before the night of the concert, I learned that Handel wrote it as an Easter offering and that its world premiere was in Dublin, Ireland, on April 13, 1742.

"Comfort ye, comfort ye my people, saith your God, saith your God," the concert began. For the next two hours, emotionally swept up in the majestic surroundings and the incredible music and the beloved story of my Christian faith, I gave no thought to the long drive back to the town where I live. As I walked to my car after the performance, I saw that a full moon had risen in the clear skies over Nashville and I smiled at the thought of it leading me home.

My smile faded as I steered my car onto the entrance ramp and timidly merged onto I-40. Three interstate highways come together in downtown Nashville, snarling traffic, confusing drivers, and causing wrecks even in daylight. After dark, it's far worse. On this holiday weekend, it was a nightmare. Hundreds of cars ahead of me. Hundreds of cars behind me. Cars to my left. Cars to my right. Cars in the lanes going the opposite direction, with only a low concrete barrier separating us. Cars entering and exiting the interstate every few hundred yards. And it wasn't just cars. Eighteen-wheelers, some of them pulling double trailers, were almost as numerous as automobiles.

That's why I was white-knuckled. That's why I was unable to hold back my tears. That's why I wished I'd never agreed to attend the Nashville Symphony, even if they were performing Handel's *Messiah* on Easter weekend.

• • •

Most times when I pray, I fold my hands, bow my head, and close my eyes. Not tonight, though. Not in the dark, going 70 miles per hour on one of the busiest interstate highways in the country. Through clenched teeth, with my breath coming shallow and my heart hammering in my chest, I prayed the same three words over and over and over again, "Help me, Lord. Help me, Lord. Help me, Lord." I didn't whisper. I didn't speak in the calm and quiet voice I normally use when I pray. Nope. I practically yelled at God, wanting to be sure He was paying attention. This was serious. I needed help right this minute!

And you know what? Right that minute, God sent help. He didn't make the traffic magically disappear. He didn't make it thin out or slow down. Instead, He directed my eyes to the back of a tractor-trailer truck only a couple of car lengths ahead of me in the right-hand lane.

The truck wasn't creeping along, but it wasn't speeding either. Four big red taillights glowed in the darkness. Smaller red lights were strung horizontally across the top of the trailer's rear doors and vertically along the sides. And here's the best part. Intersecting those doors were reflective strips, forming not an "X" but a lowercase letter "t."

The sign of the cross.

A feeling of peace descended on me. Suddenly, all my fear was gone. I knew without a doubt that the driver of this truck would lead me safely home. He would be my guardian angel. Around sharp curves and up and down the hills of Tennessee, I followed him. He never moved out of the right lane and neither did I.

About 50 miles into our journey, he slowed to a crawl and I wondered if he might be preparing to exit. Should I go around him and continue home on my own? City traffic was gone. Surely I could make it on my own now. Before I could make a move, my angel eased his truck over to straddle the dotted lines separating the lanes, making it impossible to pass on either side. I quickly discovered why. Road crews were laying fresh asphalt, taking advantage of sparse late-night traffic to perform this dangerous task.

I might have carelessly plowed ahead and caused an accident if not for my guardian angel.

A few miles beyond the paving crew, he slowed again. I soon saw the reason. A herd of white-tailed deer, their eyes shining eerily when my headlights fell upon them, were crossing the highway.

My trucker and I traveled through the night, the huge white moon lighting our way. I never tried to pass him, and he never sped away from me. We crossed over the Caney Fork River four times, and then once more as we entered the county where I live. At last, we were at my exit. My dashboard clock read 12:00. Easter Sunday, and I was safely home. I tooted my horn at my guardian angel as I pulled off the interstate and he flashed his lights at me. Then he was gone into the night.

And though I didn't fold my hands or bow my head or close my eyes as I drove the last few peaceful miles home, I prayed again. I didn't whisper. I didn't speak in a calm and quiet voice. In fact, I practically yelled three words over and over and over again, "Thank You, Lord. Thank You, Lord. Thank You, Lord."

Prayer for a Peace-Filled Life

Remind me, O God, no matter how nervous or frightened I may be, that You travel with me and send Your angels to protect me wherever I go.

Submit to God and be at peace with him; in this way prosperity will come to you.

Job 22:21 (NIV)

SUBMISSION TO GOD is difficult. We're a fiercely independent people and want to call all our own shots. That being said, our limited vision restricts what we can envision for ourselves. God sees to the horizon and beyond. He calls us to more—with the promise of more in His hands. His plan for us is so spectacular, He knows the only way to not overwhelm us with His goodness is to reveal that plan in baby steps, like He did for my friend Meghan.

When COVID hit, her husband lost his job. The hotel where he worked didn't need a manager if no one was traveling. With three kids at home, a mortgage, two car payments, and a pandemic in full swing, things became stressful. No one was hiring except the local nursing home. Meghan took the job while her husband stayed home with their kids. Someone else might have resented her circumstances: being forced to change soiled linens, clean floors and bathrooms, and do other housekeeping tasks in order to put food on the table. Yet Meghan saw it as an opportunity to submit to God's plan and bring Him to the residents.

Every chance she could, she told the residents how much God loves them. She wore silly accessories on holidays to bring cheer into their rooms and light into their hardships. It wasn't long before her fabulous attitude caught the attention of the nursing home director, who quickly promoted her to home health aide. The forward momentum didn't end there. The first time Meghan witnessed the hospice chaplain come to anoint a failing resident, she was riveted. There was something so powerful and holy about accompanying someone on their journey home to God. That's all it took for Meghan to understand why God had placed her at the nursing home—not just to earn money to pay her bills, but also to reveal her true calling. She's now enrolled in a two-year online program to become a hospice chaplain.

God has a unique plan for each one of us. We may not see the entire picture at the start. But if we trust in Him, follow His prompts, and submit to His plan, He will lead us to our purpose, where peace and prosperity abound.

—Claire McGarry

In peace I will lie down and sleep, for you alone, LORD, make me dwell in safety.

Psalm 4:8 (NIV)

PEACE IN THE NIGHT

By Haley V. Craft

AS SOON AS the words were out of my four-year-old brother's mouth, I was on board. With pouty lips and dark hazel eyes open wide to look like the saddest puppy at the pound, he'd asked the question: "Daddy, can I sleep with you tonight?"

My parents were not the kind of parents you see on reality television shows who never make their child get used to sleeping on their own. We were in our very own big-kid beds as soon as we were old enough for the shift, so it was no small feat my brother was attempting.

Heroic older sister that I was at age six, I was by his side in an instant with matching puppy-dog eyes of my own, begging Mama for the same privilege. They didn't stand a chance.

With a glance between them that a wiser person would recognize as pleased and an apparently exasperated sigh, first Daddy and then Mama relented. We were both ecstatic, running the length of the house, back and forth, in celebration of our victory and bathing the space in squeals and giggles. It was going to be the best night ever. Hands down. No contest.

As one might imagine, it took a little extra time and effort to get us ready for bed that night. A little extra wrestling with Daddy as he and Steven made their way to my parents' waterbed. An extra bedtime story from Mama before she and I headed back to my bed. But eventually we did settle down enough to climb into bed and snuggle close to our chosen parent. Lights were turned off, prayers were said, and eyes were closed—all except mine.

• • •

I had never been a child prone to falling asleep quickly. If there was someone else still up, I wanted to be in the thick of it. If there wasn't someone else up, there were plenty of imaginary adventures waiting to be had, but tonight was different.

Nobody was up. I got to sleep with Mama, which meant I got one of those gentle back scratches she'd used to lull me and Steven to sleep when we were babies. I didn't even feel the urge to go off on one of my imaginary adventures. Everything seemed to be great, a perfect storm for a quick trip to slumberland, but I couldn't find my way to rest.

As the night progressed, I noticed a feeling that hadn't been there before. It had started off small, like a whisper or the feeling of Daddy stroking my hair when I was sad. But no matter how much I tried to ignore it and go to sleep, I couldn't.

It wasn't pain or sorrow or excitement or the feeling of a little girl who just hadn't run out of energy yet. It was restlessness, the kind that comes when you feel as though something needs to be done but you have no idea what needs to be done or how to do it.

I was anxious and a little scared. Did I need to brush my teeth again? Or go to the bathroom? I didn't know why I was feeling this way. *What am I supposed to do?* The question wasn't meant for anyone in particular. It was born out of a desire to find relief by following the mysterious prompting I couldn't yet decipher. So I hadn't really expected an answer, but I got one.

It was a sense more than words that wrapped me in a sense of calm. It was like someone had offered me their hand with a smile. I couldn't see the smiling face or the outstretched hand, but I felt a presence, and with it, a silent call: *Come, Haley. Follow Me.*

• • •

I'd been in church since the womb and had heard plenty of stories about Jesus and God the Father. I didn't really understand the distinction yet, but I recognized the presence, and I felt the tension in my body ease. It was Jesus calling me. He wanted me to follow Him.

But there was a problem. How do you follow someone you can't see, hear, or physically feel? The request didn't make sense. I didn't understand. I wanted so much to do as I'd been told—that hadn't always been my MO, if I'm being honest—but now that I had the desire to follow instructions, to accept the invitation, I didn't know how.

I remember being confused as I lay there, tossing and turning, trying to work out what to do. Apparently, I tossed and turned enough to rouse Mama.

"Haley, are you OK?"

"There's something wrong with my heart." Perhaps not the best words I could have chosen. But she wasn't groggy for long.

"What's wrong? Are you in pain? Where does it hurt?"

It was too many questions too fast, and none of them were even related to what I was experiencing. I just shook my head.

"Stay right there. Be still. I'm gonna get Daddy and then we'll go see the doctor. Everything's going to be OK," she said in her best reassuring-mother voice.

"It's not that heart." She froze.

"What do you mean, 'It's not that heart'?" Mama's whole body looked rigid. It looked like she was barely breathing waiting for my answer.

"It's not the heart you go see the doctor for."

Mama paused for a moment, trying to process what I was trying to communicate.

"So it's not the heart that gives you a heartbeat?"

I shook my head.

"Is it the heart you feel happy and sad with?"

I nodded, my head down staring at the shapes the crumpled sheets made in the moonlight. It seemed silly to have woken her up and scared her because of a feeling in my heart. *Had I done something wrong?*

I felt Mama's hand on my shoulder. "What's wrong with your heart, my love?"

I don't know how I found the words to explain what I knew to be true—Jesus was calling to me and I needed to accept Him as my Lord and Savior—but somehow, she was able to understand what was going on, because a few minutes later, she had gone to find a Bible tract that presented the Gospel.

• • •

The clearest memory I have of that night is waiting while Mama went to the office to find the tract. I was sitting up in bed, the lights were on, and even though I was normally a ball of energy and only minutes ago had been a ball of nerves, now I sat in bed enveloped in a calm, quiet joy. The jumble of restlessness and fear and confusion had been washed away, leaving nothing but clear, focused peace.

Over the next few minutes, Mama shared the Gospel with me: from the beginning, when the world was perfect, to how people messed things up, and finally how Jesus had come and taken our place on the cross so we could live with Him in heaven one day. I'd heard it all before, but this time, it was different. It wasn't just individual Bible stories to me anymore. It was all connected, and it was pointing me to Jesus.

When we finished going through the tract, Mama led me through a prayer. I told Jesus that I wanted to follow Him and I wanted Him to be the Lord of my life. It was the most right-feeling thing I'd ever done, not just in the moment, but afterward as well.

A little while later, after several long hugs and a prayer of thanksgiving from Mama, we said goodnight for the second time. This time there was no restlessness. Instead, the last thing I remember about that night is experiencing a great sense of peace, a fullness of quiet joy, before I fell asleep.

Prayer for a Peace-Filled Life

Lord Jesus, when I am struggling with restlessness, please help me seek out and rest in Your perfect peace.

Yea, though I walk through the valley of the shadow of death, I will fear no evil, for You are with me. Your rod and Your staff, they comfort me.

Psalm 23:4 (NKJV)

I WILL FEAR NO EVIL

By Judith Victoria Hensley

THE WARM SUN on that September day was most welcome. A hint of fall teased the senses. My friend Rhonda had traveled the two-and-a-half-hour trip with me from home in Harlan, Kentucky, to the breast center where I would have a mammogram and ultrasound. We were looking forward to a day of shopping and a good meal in Knoxville when my appointment was complete.

My family physician had asked me to let her schedule these tests at the breast center after a recent routine exam in her office. She is an excellent physician and I try to follow any advice she gives. I believe in being proactive with health care and the ultrasound would accurately detail the lumps in my fibrocystic breasts. I had faced these concerns in past years and over time had three small lumpectomies that all proved to be benign. God had been with me at those times, and I knew He would be with me now. I trusted Him completely and knew that all would be well with me regardless of where the twists and turns of life might lead.

In the dressing room, I put on the designated black and pink robe and placed my clothes in an empty locker. When I joined the variety of women seated across the hall, we looked as if we might be scheduled for hair appointments in our matching robes. Silently we scanned magazines or cell phones, waiting for our turn. Patients moved quickly through the process.

When my name was called, I glanced at my watch and thought about where we might eat lunch. I was not thinking of the appointment as being anything other than routine. I didn't look forward to the compression of the mammogram machine, but I knew it was necessary for producing clear images of breast tissue. Focusing on making the most of a day in Knoxville kept my dread away.

After the mammogram imaging was complete, the technician asked me to return to the waiting area. I assumed the next step was having the ultrasound, and I hoped it would be less painful and just as quick. Rhonda was running an errand near the breast center, so I texted to let her know I was waiting for the ultrasound. I told her we should soon be on our way.

After the ultrasound, I was instructed to go back to the waiting room. I wondered why I couldn't get dressed and leave. A nurse appeared and called me into the hallway, informing me that the doctor wanted to repeat the ultrasound herself. Back to the waiting room I went.

The wait was growing longer than anticipated. I sent Rhonda another text advising her to go ahead and grab lunch. We could concentrate on shopping when I got out. I would grab a bite at the mall.

As I sat there, I knew there must be a problem. No one told me. I knew it in my heart. I read the statistics on a poster in the waiting room, "One in eight women will be diagnosed with breast cancer." I'd read this before and always wondered which one of my friends it might be. That day, I knew the one in eight was going to be me. Eventually I was called in for the second ultrasound.

• • •

The awareness of the pending diagnosis should have terrified me. My best friend from high school had died from breast cancer. Another acquaintance had lost her battle after years of treatments and surgeries. Instead of fear, however, peace settled over my spirit, my heart, and my mind, as if God Himself wrapped me in a warm blanket of comfort.

As clearly as I have ever heard anything in my spirit, I heard the message: "Judy, you are going to have to walk through the valley of the shadow of death, but I will be with you every step of the way."

I pondered this in my heart. I didn't know what was ahead, but I trusted God's words. This diagnosis would not be the one that signaled my time on earth to be fulfilled. I knew this beyond a shadow of a doubt.

I prayed that God would give me strength to endure whatever was ahead and to use this season of my life as an opportunity to share my faith with others. The sense of peace grew even deeper. God was not a liar. The Holy Spirit would not have spoken so clearly to me in a falsehood. The Comforter had already poured His peace into me.

Even when the doctor completed her scan and asked me to stay for a biopsy as soon as she could get back to me, peace remained, and it was well with my soul. No one had spoken the "C" word to me at that point. No one indicated their suspicion that had resulted in an urgent arrangement for a biopsy, which required an assistant and the doctor to stay past clinic hours to get it done.

When the doctor gave me the news after the procedure, she was filled with compassion. I felt compassion back for her, realizing that delivering such life-altering news to patients was part of her daily routine. I asked the basic questions, and she recommended a surgeon and set the gears in motion to get a surgical date.

I can't say that my mind wasn't racing in many directions with thoughts of negative scenarios. This would be an interruption in the life I had planned. I knew I would be facing a future that was different than I expected, but I also knew that God held that future in His loving hands.

Rhonda, of course, knew something was amiss because of the hours that had passed from the time I went in for the appointment and the time I walked back out the front door, but I decided not to tell anyone else about my situation. My mother was experiencing heart issues, my dad had been through colon cancer a year earlier, my son was experiencing challenges in his own life, and my brother lived out of town and had his hands full with work. They could not change the situation, so I chose not to burden them with it.

I also didn't want this news to become a topic of compassionate gossip. I didn't want anyone to speak death over me. The power of life and death is in the tongue, so there would be no speaking death if no one knew what was going on. I waited until the week before surgery to ask my close circle of friends and family to pray for me. I did not tell them I'd already had the diagnosis but told them only that I had a lump that had to be removed.

Rhonda, her husband, and my son were with me the day of the surgery. Both my breasts were altered and reconstructed during this single operation, with the surgeon doing the removal and the plastic surgeon doing the reconstruction. I didn't realize until much later what an incredible miracle this was in itself.

Healing from the surgery took a while, followed by weeks of radiation. During my treatment, I became acutely aware of women around me who had to face the same long valley. I encountered women of great faith and women filled with fear and despair. Through it all, the gift of God's peace never wavered in me, and it's a gift I was able to share with others in an arena I had never anticipated.

Prayer for a Peace-Filled Life

Father, You know our mortal lives are full of shadowy places and unspoken fears. I ask that You shine the light of Your love in these dark places and dispel both the shadow and fear they generate. Our trust is in You, as You walk with us and comfort us in every situation we must face. Help us to embrace Your peace that passes understanding. Amen.

Finally, brothers and sisters, rejoice, mend your ways, be comforted, be like-minded, live in peace; and the God of love and peace will be with you.

2 Corinthians 13:11 (NASB)

WILDFLOWER LOVE

By Lynne Hartke

"WHAT ARE YOUR FAVORITE FLOWERS?" my husband Kevin asked me while we were both trying to get out the door one busy morning. I thought the query a bit odd. After almost four decades of marriage, didn't he know the answer?

"Whatever flowers you give me," I replied, an answer I had given multiple times throughout the years. Whether the flowers had been red roses, carnations, or cut daisies, it didn't matter. Whenever I received flowers from my husband for birthdays, anniversaries, important milestones, or "just because," I had declared them to be my favorites.

But the reason for the question became known several weeks later, when Kevin presented me with a massive bouquet at our fortieth anniversary celebration. Wanting to cover all the bases, Kevin had asked the florist to choose ten varieties of pink or red flowers in groups of four. Delicate hydrangeas, pink stargazer lilies, large gerbera daisies, pink roses, and red carnations filled the container.

The vase was so large that I needed both hands to hold all that romantic love as we posed for photo after photo.

"Oh darling," I exclaimed, "these are my favorite!"

• • •

I thought of those flowers months later as we arrived at our cabin in northern Arizona for a weekend getaway. Since our anniversary celebration, the days had not included many flowers or gestures of romance. Rather, our time and calendar had been consumed with an election campaign for Kevin's second term as mayor, a job he held while also serving part-time as a pastor. He had been on an exhaustive pace for months, attending rallies, meet-and-greet events, and debates, not only for himself, but also for several candidates he was endorsing. In addition, the pace of my life had also increased, with multiple speaking trips away from home.

We needed the time away with just the two of us. I had high expectations for the weekend: a long walk together in the woods, a quiet romantic dinner, and intimate conversation by the fireplace. We would be together and do all the together things. That was the plan, at least in my mind.

My expectations began to unravel minutes after we finished unloading the car.

"I'm going for a walk," Kevin announced after placing the cooler—the last item from the car—on the kitchen counter. "I'll be back in a bit."

Before I could respond and grab my shoes, he was gone. He even left behind our rust-colored mutt, Mollie. Dejected, she plopped down next to the closed door, an echo of my own disappointment.

"Well, so much for expectation number one," I muttered. "Come on, Mollie, let's go for our own walk."

Tail wagging, she joined me for a stroll on the property. An abundance of end-of-summer rains had brought out the wildflowers. Several bluebonnets clung to the cliff edge. A hummingbird hovered near a firecracker penstemon, while his mate sampled the nectar in the trumpet flowers of a scarlet gilia. Mollie dug her nose under an old log, jostling a purple tansyaster. Wildflowers were everywhere, enticing me with their fragile beauty as they invited me to marvel at their ability to grow in unexpected places.

On the way back to the cabin, I set in motion the second part of the plan—a romantic fire in the fireplace. Mollie followed me to the cedar, aspen, and pine logs stacked next to the back deck. As I balanced kindling, pine cones, and small logs in my arms, I checked my watch. An hour had passed. I had assumed Kevin would take a short loop of the neighborhood and then return home. Where could he be?

In the kitchen, I threw Mollie a doggy treat, while I marinated the steaks, rubbing in salt, pepper, and minced garlic. I sliced brussels sprouts—Kevin's favorite—and tossed them in olive oil. After sharing my husband with a city and a church, I had looked forward to a quiet evening meal. I had told myself we would connect at the cabin, but with each passing minute, I had to face the fact that my expectations might not be met.

• • •

Where can he be? I wondered again after another hour had passed. Mollie kept watch with me while I started the fire in the fireplace, the flames chasing off the chill of the growing darkness. The light could not dispel my rising concern.

Could he have fallen off the cliff edge? Been bitten by a rattlesnake? And what about that mountain lion a neighbor had reported? Was it back in the neighborhood?

My mind raced in all directions.

Then my worry refocused as anger. Didn't he realize I had plans? Expectations? I would give him a piece of my mind when he walked in the door!

Enough!

The unspoken word held the scolding tone of a librarian. But rather than a word of caution regarding noise level in a room filled with books, I knew the word was spoken by the Spirit of God to calm the noise level in my mind. My expectations and focus on possible disasters had allowed my worry and anger to spiral out of control, robbing me of my peace.

After all, I was being ridiculous. After forty years of marriage, I was familiar with my husband's adventuresome spirit. When life became overwhelming, he needed space to recalibrate. After shouldering the concerns of a small congregation and the responsibility of a city of 280,000 people, he needed time wandering alone in the woods before he could be fully present to me.

Kevin would show up soon, unscathed and ready for an evening together. If I didn't get my expectations under control, the evening would be ruined.

As I put the finishing touches on dinner, I prayed Kevin would find relief from the tension while he walked among the ponderosa pines under the watchful eyes of Steller's jays, curious mountain chickadees, and ground squirrels. As I prayed, I remembered Kevin not only walked under the eyes of the wildlife, but he also walked with Jesus, who loved him.

And me. Who loved me.

A few minutes later, Mollie ran to the back door, her dog tags jingling. Her canine ears had detected the sound of someone on the deck. Kevin was back!

He met me at the door with a boyish grin. And not just a grin. In his hands, he held a jumbled bouquet of wildflowers—a mix of Indian paintbrush, scarlet gilia, yellow snapdragons, and purple tansyasters.

"I was getting worried," I confessed as I placed the flowers in a quart jar. "You were gone so long."

"I needed to clear my head."

I nodded. I understood.

We sat down to a quiet dinner by the fireplace. We talked about things that mattered. About the future. About us. About carving time away.

I knew my prayer had paved the way for a peaceful evening, but it also opened my eyes to something unexpected. I had come with the plan for a weekend getaway, but instead of huge, romantic gestures—like a vase overflowing with greenhouse flowers—love found us in small, spontaneous ways. Wildflower love.

The next day, Kevin kissed the back of my neck while he made coffee in the kitchen. He washed the dishes after our pancake breakfast. He stacked the wood by the fireplace, so I didn't need to go outside to gather kindling. And each time I passed the wildflowers in the glass quart jar on the fireplace mantel, I thought of my husband gathering them for me as he walked in the woods.

I touched the slender petals.

They are my favorite.

Prayer for a Peace-Filled Life

Jesus, when my inner narrative tells me a story that is not true, open my eyes to see love and peace blooming in beautiful ways right in front of me. Amen.

Nevertheless, I will bring health and healing to it; I will heal my people and will let them enjoy abundant peace and security.

Jeremiah 33:6 (NIV)

JESUS HEALED WHEREVER He went (Matthew 4:23). Knowing this, people flocked to Him, laying the sick in the marketplace, begging Him to let them touch even the edge of His cloak (Mark 6:56). When the crowds were too large to get to Him, some friends of a paralytic even made a hole in the roof of the house where Jesus was and then lowered the man down to Him. Jesus's first reaction wasn't to heal the man's physical condition though. It was to heal the condition of his soul. It wasn't until after He forgave the paralytic's sins that Jesus cured the man (Mark 2:1–13).

The condition of our soul is always God's first priority. His Word tells us that it's the only thing that truly matters. Our bodies are temporal. His kingdom is eternal. What He yearns for most is for us to be righteous and true so we'll reside one day in heaven with Him. Deacon Leland, from my church, and his wife, Michelle, understand this well.

They recently took a year to travel the country. They didn't call it a vacation because their focus wasn't on enjoyment. They called it a "pilgrimage" because they were on a quest to find out what God wanted from them next. When that year ended, they discerned that they were called to return to our parish and serve.

A few months later, Deacon Leland was diagnosed with multiple myeloma. Although he's undergoing treatments in hopes that the cancer will be cured, he recognizes that he already received a healing while on his pilgrimage—that of his soul. The resulting and unwavering surrender to God's will is what is empowering him and Michelle to face his diagnosis head-on, with irrevocable peace in their hearts, no matter what happens.

We all have something we struggle with. Whether it's a physical or mental illness, or some other insurmountable burden, it's not unusual to wonder why God allows us to suffer. Yet God moves in miraculous ways. He is always at the ready to heal whoever turns to Him. In fact, healings happen all the time. Some are healed physically; others are healed spiritually, with the only visible sign being the serenity in their eyes. They are the ones who find tranquility in the midst of their trial by inviting God into it. Knowing He's walking with them through it all brings an abiding peace, no matter the outcome for their body.

—Claire McGarry

I have told you these things, so that in me you may have peace. In this world you will have trouble. But take heart! I have overcome the world.

John 16:33 (NIV)

PEACE OF MIND, BODY, AND SOUL

By Eryn Lynum

MY HAND TREMBLED as I grasped the doorknob on our front door. In fact, walking into our home with my four young children trailing behind, my entire body was shaking from fear and exhaustion.

"Mom, I'll get everyone fed for dinner and into bed." At ten years old, my firstborn seemed older than his age as he prepared peanut butter sandwiches for his three younger siblings. Meanwhile, I retreated to my bedroom and collapsed into bed. At last, behind a closed door and out of sight of my children, I let my tears flow freely.

An hour before, we'd left my husband at the hospital. What we thought was a common illness turned into an admission into the hospital and immediate rounds of antibiotics and medications. Shocked at the nurse's pronouncement, I had taken the children home alone. We were exhausted and needed rest, although I knew I would not be sleeping that night.

I felt weak as I rose from my bed and stared out the window. The sun had fallen below the horizon. It was late, and hollow loneliness heightened my fear. I could hear my children shuffling around upstairs now, preparing for bed. I dialed the hospital phone number and waited for the nurse to pick it up.

"I'm looking for an update on my husband," I explained, my voice cracking.

"We've administered the first round of antibiotics," the nurse calmly explained, and then added, "We just need to get him through this."

I thanked her, hung up, then walked down the hallway to kiss my children goodnight.

Lord, I prayed after the kids were tucked in, *I need rest.*

• • •

I wasn't sure what tomorrow would bring—only that I would need to remain strong for my sons and daughter. But fear had punctured my faith, and anxiety sapped every ounce of strength out of me. I felt like the Apostle Paul in 2 Corinthians 1:8 (ESV), "For we were so utterly burdened beyond our strength…"

I texted a dear friend, and she immediately called back.

"Can I pray with you?" she asked as soon as I picked up. She prayed for my husband's healing and peace for the kids and me. Yes—peace. Peace is what I needed, but a more profound peace than I had ever experienced. I had never known a fear like this—so consuming and entirely outside of my control. Only supernatural peace could conquer it. I needed perfect, all-encompassing peace—the kind I'd read about in Scripture but always through a haze. For twenty-six years, I'd followed Christ as my Savior, but this level of peace I'd always heard about felt elusive.

I had read about peace beyond measure in Philippians 4:7 (NIV): "And the peace of God, which transcends all understanding, will guard your hearts and your minds in Christ Jesus." And yet, the peace that transcends all understanding always seemed to also exceed my grasp. It felt like a facet of the faith journey I'd never truly understood or experienced. I knew this peace only comes from God. It is the perfect peace God promises in Isaiah 26:3 (NIV): "You will keep in perfect peace those whose minds are steadfast, because they trust in you."

But what makes peace *perfect*? What sets it aside as holy, complete, and sourced in God? I began to understand that perfect peace can only stem from perfect love—like a tree producing the fruit of its own kind. I could draw a direct line from perfect peace back to perfect love, a love which, as 1 John 4:18 (ESV) promises, "casts out fear."

I whispered a prayer, *Lord, I need Your peace like I've never experienced before.*

Perhaps I did not know exactly what I was asking for, because I had never experienced it. However, there is power in praying in line with God's promises. I trusted that as my prayers cooperated with His truth, they would unleash the living and active power of His Word. I was confident He has a reservoir of this perfect peace and is simply waiting for me to draw from it.

• • •

As I prayed, a profound calmness settled over my mind and body. It enveloped me and subdued my fearful thoughts. Moments before, anxious scenarios had filled my mind. Now, even as I tried to mentally reach back and grasp those thoughts, I could not. The questions that had run on repeat since the hospital were now fractured.

"What if he..."

"What about the kids..."

"Will the doctors be able to..."

My fearful thoughts were unreachable—severed like a broken chain. This peace did not make sense. But then, that's precisely what God promises me: peace beyond comprehension. Jesus spoke of this unworldly peace in John 14:27 (NIV), "Peace I leave with you; my peace I give you. I do not give to you as the world gives. Do not let your hearts be troubled and do not be afraid."

Later in my faith journey, I would come to a deeper understanding of this indescribable peace I was experiencing. I would realize that the roots of the Hebrew word not only allude to complete peace of mind and soul but are also a physical remedy. It is defined by a "soundness of body." My heart—fatigued from pounding hard in my chest—slackened its anxious beating. Both my mind and body relaxed, and I fell quickly into a deep, restful sleep.

• • •

Dawn brought new morning mercies and renewed strength. I texted my husband, then let out a breath of relief when I saw the blinking dots on the screen signaling that he was typing back. He answered that he was doing better. To be sure, I called the nurse, and she confirmed that the treatments were working.

God's peace steadied me as we waited for further updates throughout the day. His peace also strengthened my mind, equipping me to take every fearful thought captive and have a mind "stayed on Thee." His promise of peace is often paired with strength, like in Psalm 29:11 (NKJV), "The Lord will give strength to His people; The Lord will bless His people with peace." When His peace unwinds fear's tendrils from my spirit, He restores me by His power.

I'm finding this to be true not only in tragedy but also in everyday circumstances. Fear and worry routinely whittle away at my endurance. I exhaust myself with thoughts running in cyclical patterns. These well-worn ruts of anxious notions erode my resolve, leaving me weak and vulnerable to more fear. And yet, as I realized when my husband was hospitalized, God's reservoir of peace never runs dry—not when I take a big draw, such as in calamity, nor in the slow and steady flow sustaining me daily. His peace is sufficient.

Two days after my husband was admitted into the hospital, we picked him up and brought him home to recover. He was terribly weak. But I knew that just as God had strengthened me, He would strengthen my husband also. I was grateful not only to have my husband back but also to have a new perspective on God's nearness and an intimate experience with His perfect peace.

Since then, I have continued to experience God's peace on an ever-deepening level, knowing it is truly inexhaustible and readily available. I view it as an ocean with depths I have yet to discover. Throughout my life, I've stood at the ocean's edge many times and marveled at its mysteries. To date, science has mapped less than a quarter of the ocean floor. What might there be to discover in such vast expanses and depths?

God's peace is similar. So much of it, I've never breached the surface of. And yet, through my husband's illness and recovery, I realized that God is inviting me into new depths of peace like I've never known before. I can experience His perfect and indescribable peace in my mind, body, and soul.

Prayer for a Peace-Filled Life

Dear God, Your peace is beyond description. I know I have yet to experience even a small portion of all it offers. Help me to draw on Your perfect peace daily and to trust that it is more than enough for my mind, body, and soul.

So do not fear, for I am with you; do not be dismayed, for I am your God. I will strengthen you and help you; I will uphold you with my righteous right hand.

Isaiah 41:10 (NIV)

STRENGTH IN PEACE

By Cristina Moore

MY HUSBAND, ROB, and I both served in the national guard. I'd been serving stateside to keep everything running at home. Rob had been deployed to Iraq for a year and had just returned home when he received his assignment to serve in the same unit with me. Although it was not unheard of for a husband and wife to serve in the same unit, it was not common.

My role in the guard was as a company commander. This meant that I led the team that provided all support functions for the brigade, from food to maintenance of vehicles. Our entire company was a little more than 250, with a large number of officers serving as staff within the brigade.

Shortly after, we received word that our company would be the next to go to Iraq. Our orders indicated we would serve in Iraq, leading the engineering efforts on both combat and construction missions. This meant that we would not only serve in the same unit, but that we also would deploy together to a combat zone. Our commander sat us down and asked us if one of us wanted to remain behind and not deploy. Although the risk was great for one or both of us to get injured or not return home, we didn't hesitate. Our answer was "no." Deploying was our job, our mission. We couldn't ask others to serve in our place simply because we were married.

As we readied to deploy, I was moved from my command post to serve in the operations section. This section consisted of two groups—one that planned the missions while the other executed the plans. My husband was part of the planning group.

One of our company's requirements was to provide security for all convoy operations. Simply put, anytime vehicles left our base, this hand-selected group of soldiers would provide gun security to help support a safe passage. Our location in Iraq was known for the enemy placing improvised explosive devices (IEDs) along the routes to disrupt movement. These devices not only led to the damage of countless military vehicles and equipment, but they also were the leading cause of our military's injuries and deaths. Rob was designated the leader of this security team.

My job was to run the day-to-day operations of our unit. That meant I served as a "battle captain" that stayed on base and tracked and supported all ongoing missions. I would track every convoy that left the base and track all construction projects and other missions across Iraq. The job was far from routine, but every day began to blend into the next as I counted down the days until Rob and I would return home. At least that was the case until that fateful day when not only was my faith tested, but also when I felt an inexplicable peace in the midst of my greatest fear.

• • •

That morning, Rob was running security for a convoy leaving the base. He had completed similar missions countless times, and I knew his team was well trained. They had trained to the point that all their actions were muscle memory. I was not unnecessarily worried when Rob moved to lead his convoy while I moved to start my day in the operations center. I knew I would see him when he returned.

My normal routine in the mornings was to grab coffee with my boss and one of my noncommissioned officers—a routine we had followed for countless days while in Iraq. As we were walking to the operations center, my boss took a call. I saw his steps falter before he quickly recovered and responded cryptically to the voice on the other line. I sensed that something was not quite right. He pulled me aside before I could enter the operations center and let me know that we'd lost contact with my husband's convoy. They had hit an IED.

I felt a loud ringing in my ears as I lost track of time and my surroundings. *There must be a mistake*, I thought. They'd just left the base. My eyes began to fill with tears as I looked at my boss and nodded my head slightly to let him know I acknowledged what he had just said. He placed his hand on my arm and gently squeezed as I tried to grasp what this meant. I couldn't remember what my last words were to my husband that morning. Had I told him I loved him? Was that the last time I would see his smile or hear his voice?

I told my boss I needed a minute and walked into an empty office. I felt my entire body shake as I feared the worst. No words came from my lips, but silent prayers cascaded in my mind. I couldn't formulate or voice a coherent prayer; I simply asked God to help me, over and over in my mind. My hand grasped the corner of the desk so I wouldn't collapse as I felt the overwhelming weight of loss and struggled to breathe through my uncontrollable tears. What could I do? How could I fix this?

In what felt like a lifetime but was only minutes, I began to feel a calm and peace slowly pass through my body as my breathing began to slow. God had heard my unspoken prayers. There was nothing I could do; I could not fix this. But I knew God had me and would guide me in my next steps. I was not alone. His strength was my strength.

• • •

I took several deep breaths and wiped away my tears. Just as my husband had conducted his mission, I had to do mine. I walked to the operations center, quickly assessed the situation, and started the tasks of routing the convoy home. We had to get everyone back inside the base.

Once the convoy was back, I headed to meet them at the hospital. I didn't know if I would find my husband injured or dead. I didn't dare to hope. When I arrived at the hospital, I recognized several of his team but I didn't see him. I finally drew the courage to ask where he was and if he was OK. That's when I saw him walking out of the hospital with blood on his body armor. I learned the blood wasn't his. My husband had provided lifesaving aid to a soldier who'd been thrown from a vehicle, and it was that soldier's blood. Everyone came back alive. They were safe.

That day, I not only felt God through prayer, but I also felt Him surround me and hold me close. I felt His strength when I had none; I felt His peace when I was consumed by fear. Ever since that day, whenever I feel loss or sorrow, fear or worry, I pray and God gives me peace.

Prayer for a Peace-Filled Life

Lord, help me to remember to turn to You in prayer to find peace and calm when I am consumed and frozen by fear or anxiety.

In my Father's house are many mansions: if it were not so, I would have told you. I go to prepare a place for you.

John 14:2 (KJV)

WHEN WORDS FAIL

By Sylvia Gardner

MY DEAR FRIENDS' mother had passed away, and their despondent father, Jim, suffered a stroke and a bad fall two hours afterward. I was beside myself with sadness. I just had to do something to help Jim and the rest of the family. Something that went beyond the typical flowers and casseroles.

I prayed about it, and finally an idea came to me. While Jim's four adult children attended their mother's funeral, I would stay with their father in his hospital room.

• • •

I'm a nurse practitioner, and I first met Jim years earlier after relocating from upstate New York to rural Kentucky. When I visited him in his home, he was having a flare-up of his emphysema and was scared half to death. After I listened to his heart and lungs, I decided to let him rest a bit. "Would it be all right if I stopped on my way home from the hospital tomorrow to check on you again?" I asked.

"I wouldn't care a bit," Jim said between labored breaths.

Crushed at his response, I turned to his wife, whom he called Bunny Pie. "I guess I won't be seeing you either," I said quietly. "He doesn't want me to come back."

She scrunched her face into a giant question mark, then a grin eased itself across her delicate features. "Oh, Jim just meant he'd be pleased as punch to have you back, Miss Syl!"

It was one of my first lessons on figures of speech in the hills of Appalachia. Back where I come from, Jim's comment meant a person didn't want to do something.

Over the next couple of decades, Jim, Bunny Pie, and I became great buddies, as well as experts in speaking the same language. We learned we had all been raised on farms and valued honest hard work. Jim and Bunny Pie admired my take-charge way of doing things too. When Jim was diagnosed with prostate cancer that had spread to his bones, I helped him figure out how to manage his pain. And when Bunny Pie's breast cancer returned, I was there for her.

I couldn't abandon them now. The least I could do is go be with Jim during his beloved wife's funeral.

• • •

On that April afternoon, an hour before Bunny Pie's service was to begin, I paused in the lobby of St. Mary's Hospital to study a child's construction-paper angel tacked onto a bulletin board. The celestial being's exaggerated facial features and garish crayon colors reminded me of similar projects my own two kids had once completed at our kitchen table. Yet a strange feeling overcame me, and try as I might, I couldn't turn away from the ordinary drawing. As my fingers traced the curlicues on the angel's flowing magenta gown, my eyes fell upon a small white card pinned to it. I read its message written in black calligraphy: "The Christian life is one of action, not speech and daydreams. Let there be few words and many deeds, and let them be done well."

I glanced at the manila folder in my hand that contained all the words I'd intended to say to Jim about Bunny Pie. I'd waxed on about her roles as a wife, a mother, a caretaker of shut-ins on her block. How even when the two of them had both faced cancers spreading to their bones, they had looked after each other in their own home. A home where Bunny Pie had been able to stay until two weeks before her death.

Now my words seemed totally inadequate. A voice spoke to my spirit: *The crayon angel is right, Sylvia. Let somebody else do the talking for once. You just focus on actions.*

As I boarded the hospital elevator to the fifth floor, my plan consumed me. Lo and behold, I overheard one of the Catholic sisters and a chaplain conversing quietly in back of me. It was just the three of us, and I found myself turning to address them as if we'd known each other for years. "A friend of mine is a patient here," I said. "He lost his wife, and all the family is at the funeral right now. He's too sick to be with them. Any chance you could assist me with a little remembrance of her in his hospital room?"

"I'm Sister Joanne," the lady answered in the gentlest voice. "And I certainly don't see why not." Mercy flowed from her very being.

Then the chaplain spoke up. "Now, I'm new here," he said, "but I'll do anything I can to help." He said his name was John.

When the three of us arrived on the fifth floor, we headed toward Jim's private room at the end of a long corridor. On the way, I noticed a blonde nurse with her medication cart. She was the most joyful little thing, and as she rolled along, she ever-so-softly sang the old Dolly Parton tune that Whitney Houston had recently made popular: "I Will Always Love You." Her lilting soprano voice enchanted me.

The nurse's name tag said "Patty," and I quickly explained my plan to her. "But the thing is, we need some music, Patty. Any chance you know 'In the Garden' and could spare a few minutes?"

Patty confided that Jim was one of her favorite patients and that she would be honored to oblige. She said she sang "In the Garden" at her church and would find us as soon as she passed out her meds.

• • •

Outside Jim's room, the four of us paused at a large plate-glass window. Yellow daffodils dotted the hospital grounds. We watched as a young couple, hand in hand, headed for the parking lot. *Jim and Bunny Pie in earlier days,* I thought. *How he loved her.*

The chaplain prayed for God's guidance in our efforts to comfort Jim. When we entered his room, I was heartbroken to see him all bruised and with broken bones. He looked so alone and small in that hospital bed, his eyes glazed over. "While your family is at your wife's funeral, we thought we'd be with *you* for a few moments," the chaplain explained.

I took Jim's frail hand and propped a framed picture of Bunny Pie on his overbed table. "We'll just 'sit a spell,' as you always say," I told him.

"Don't count on *him* to say anything," the lady pushing a mop in Jim's bathroom called out. "Been here since he came in, and he ain't spoke nary a word. The stroke, I gather."

Sister Joanne's soft voice began: "For He shall give His angels charge over thee, to keep thee in all thy ways."

Next Patty began her rendition of "In the Garden." Her soprano was even lovelier than I imagined, hearing her there in the hallway. As she sang, a smile slowly found its way across Jim's battered face. When she got to the line "And He tells me I am His own," he began to nod.

Now it was time for Chaplain John to read from God's Word. Just then, he realized he didn't have his Bible with him. "There's always one in this stand," Patty said, jiggling the metal drawer. But her search came up empty.

Chaplain John began to recite from memory the Scripture from John 14:2 (KJV). "This is the Lord's promise, Jim," he said. "In my Father's house are many mansions. . ."

He stopped abruptly, then repeated the words, for emphasis I thought. I noticed that his face was flushed, and he was shaking his head and staring at his shoes. "I've known that verse for years," he muttered. "But I can't recall the rest of it now."

A different voice suddenly broke the silence. One that was quiet and measured, growing surer with every word.

Jim's!

"If. It. Were. Not. So. I. Would. Have. Told. You," he said, completing the verse. His head stretched toward the heavens and a peaceful glow brightened his stubbly face. "I. Go. To. Prepare. A. Place. For. You."

My heart was so filled with awe, I could barely breathe. We all paused for a few moments, then the chaplain concluded our little remembrance with a prayer. I gave Jim a long goodbye hug and promised to visit him again soon. As I left the hospital, I knew for all time that when words fail us, if we offer our best love, the angels take care of the rest.

After Jim was discharged from the hospital and was recovering at the rehab center, I stopped in to see him. We got to reminiscing about his wife's impromptu service. "Don't reckon I'd be talking today, Miss Syl, if that parson you recruited hadn't forgotten his Bible," Jim said with a wistful chuckle. "I just couldn't let my Bunny Pie go to live with the angels without a proper funeral."

Prayer for a Peace-Filled Life

While our words may fail and be fleeting, Lord, Yours are just what we need. Thank You for Your peace-filled promise of a forever home with You.

He will wipe every tear from their eyes. There will be no more death or mourning or crying or pain, for the old order of things has passed away.

Revelation 21:4 (NIV)

WHEN SOMEONE WE LOVE passes away, it cracks our heart in two. The ache of missing them makes it impossible to imagine life without them. With every holiday and milestone thereafter, we feel the void where they should be.

We forget that one man, Adam, brought death into the world, yet another man, Christ, brought new life. It was by His sacrifice that our loved ones are resurrected and live in the presence of God, where there is no more pain, no more suffering, no more want. We have to be willing to think of them there in order for our hearts to heal.

Author Brian Charles lost his mother to lung cancer when he was only twenty-two years old. While steeped in grief, he had a vivid dream where she came to him and said, "I'm OK." He recalls that when he woke, he was filled with a peace and certainty that she was in a better place, whole and happy, no longer in a wheelchair from the stroke she'd suffered, her speech restored and her body healed. He imagined her dancing and free, possessing joy for all eternity.

We may not have a dream where a deceased loved one visits us to say, "I'm OK." But we do have a God that gave us His only begotten Son so that those who believe in Him will live forever (John 3:16). That promise is far more concrete than any dream we could ever have. Through it comes a surety that those we love have had their bodies restored to perfection "in the twinkling of an eye" (1 Corinthians 15:52, NIV) and they are now able to see the face of God (Job 19:27). The thought of them dancing in His presence, free from illness, pain, or want should wipe away every tear we've shed. For all eternity, they'll be dwelling where the sun or moon have no need to shine because the glory of God lights it (Revelation 21:23).

Being a citizen in the presence of God is far greater than just being OK. It's one all Christians long for. Knowing our loved ones have gone to their eternal and perfect home is a promise fulfilled, bringing deep peace and endless joy.

—Claire McGarry

Trust in the Lord with all your heart and lean not on your own understanding; in all your ways submit to Him, and He will make your paths straight.

Proverbs 3:5–6 (NIV)

BUTTERFLIES AND BREAD

By Judi Logan

BUTTERFLIES! BEAUTIFUL BUTTERFLIES! Even though it was the middle of March in New Jersey, I stared up at the ceiling from my hospital bed, working very hard to picture butterflies. In my teens, on a very difficult day, a butterfly fluttered right in front of my eyes and lifted my spirits. From that time on, I clung to the life cycle of butterflies as a means of hope when life was hardest.

When I was younger, I'd spend many days crawling around in the dirt, seeing only a caterpillar on the underside of flowers or a dark cocoon attached there. The beauty wouldn't unfold until days later. Today, it seemed my efforts were repeating history, as I couldn't conjure anything beautiful on that ceiling. In my mind's eye, I could only see yet another period of challenge and change.

I'd been battling a chronic illness for many months, and this was my second stay at the hospital in the past few months. Although this was pre-COVID, my immune system was too weak to allow many visitors. I was blessed with family and friends who called and texted often, and I knew, in the deepest part of me, that the Lord was with me every step of the way, even this day, when I struggled with self-pity. In between IV refills, blood draws, and all of the annoying parts of hospitalization, my mind spent hours trying to soothe my unrest, rerunning examples of recent times when difficult and dark eventually grew bright. I was certain that remembering all that history would reignite my faith light.

• • •

Five years earlier, I'd lost my husband, Jack. He'd casually tossed his golf bag in the car and headed to the golf course. At the end of nine holes of fun-in-the-sun, surrounded by three of his best friends-in-the-Son, he collapsed. When I got to the hospital and learned his heart attack had been fatal, I knew without a shadow of a doubt that Jack was joyfully with Jesus. But while that knowledge was truly comforting, the claws of grief gripped me tightly.

As the days and weeks passed, I continued to feel blindsided by this unexpected solo dance and struggled to find my way around life's darkened dance floor. For many reasons, my day-to-day grew very complicated. My prayer—sometimes hourly—was "Trust in the LORD with all your heart and lean not on your own understanding." Every day—every single day—I thanked God for amazing family and friends who cared so selflessly and continuously for me. But it took me months before I awakened one day and could really see a shimmer of light way off in the distance.

I'd been sorting papers from Jack's desk when I discovered an article he'd saved about Horatio G. Spafford's hymn "It Is Well with My Soul." Spafford's inspiration to write a praise song when the ship in which he was traveling precisely crossed the location of the shipwreck that had taken the lives of his children shone light into my darkness. *The* Light! Just as the timing of Spafford's inspiration was clearly God's work, I was certain the timing of my discovery of that story could not have been coincidental. I could feel God's presence like never before. And just as Spafford's hymn validates loss and pain while clearly focusing on God's constant love and presence, I became acutely aware of those truths in my struggles.

• • •

With each new awareness, the light in my twisting tunnel kept growing bigger and closer. Lean not on my own understanding. Trust God to carry me through! Perhaps this deepening faith was the reward for enduring the hard. Such a difference for me to sing "It Is Well with My Soul" when I knew the spirit behind it and fully believed it! Such joy when I reached the end of a tunnel! I prayed for ways to bring light into every place I went and heart I met. I didn't stop missing Jack, but I stopped missing opportunities to love and serve.

And then suddenly, I was back in a new tunnel. Ten months after Jack's death, I was diagnosed with breast cancer. At the anniversary of his passing, I placed his favorite orange and pink roses in the memorial garden and prepared for my upcoming mastectomy. Family and friends were still lifting and loving me without missing a beat, and I was beyond grateful, fully aware that God was driving this team. But it was bewildering that with all of those earth angels beside me, I was yet again plunged into a sea of fog and fear. "Trust in the LORD with all your heart and lean not on your own understanding." I was back to praying these words from Proverbs repeatedly, convinced this latest darkness was a clear indication I hadn't done as great a job of growing my faith as I'd thought.

It took close to a year to get through the surgeries and treatments, but along the way, I met amazing people, including other cancer survivors and caring medical professionals. Each brought bouquets of friendship, laughter, and understanding I might never have had if I'd escaped this journey. In retrospect, I could see the "caterpillars" and the "cocoons" in that life tunnel, but also the utter joy shining from all those "butterflies" dancing in the sun with me. I wallowed in butterflies for quite a while and finally was able to jump back into sharing love and joy whenever I could.

• • •

Until I couldn't. A long-in-remission illness reared its ugly head, sending me into hallways of flu-crowded emergency rooms and inpatient wards, where personnel were stressed beyond the max. It was a perfect place for darkness to reenter and build walls around the Light. My "trust in the Lord" mantra was apparently hibernating, and I couldn't seem to remember the tune to "It Is Well with My Soul," much less the words.

Once back home, medications and continued symptoms kept me isolated for many more weeks and that dark wall just seemed to get thicker. I remained unable to get a glimpse of the Light. I knew it was there; I just needed to find it. Frustrated one morning, I yelled into the empty house, "I need help!" Instantly I sensed an answer. I didn't hear actual words; just a thought, loud in my mind: *Make bread!*

Yes, from-scratch bread baking, just like I'd done every week when raising my family. I had yelled "need," but my brain registered "knead." Ridiculous as it seemed, I knew that while I was absorbed in the process of creating bread from flour, water, and yeast, my mind and hands would be too busy for darkness to crowd in. As I mixed the dough and set it for the first rising, I realized there would be far too many loaves for me to consume, and the idea for Blessings

Bread was born. I spent the rising time making labels to put on the wrapped loaves I would give to my angel helpers.

Punching the air out of the raised lump, I felt a strange release, like a fresh breeze blown into my soul. Kneading the dough brought memories into my fingers. Closing my eyes, I pressed and turned the dough as automatically and rhythmically as I'd done all those decades ago.

• • •

Making bread had been a serene break during those busy-mom times; with each press and turn that day, calmness gently whispered the darkness away. I began to think about the connection between kneading bread and needing God. How the dough has to go through darkness and fire before it can nourish and sustain. How Jesus, the Bread of Life, suffered and was broken—to nourish and sustain us!

Overcome with so many connections between my bread project and the presence of God's love filling my heart and home, I felt urgency to move onto my back porch. I tenderly placed the loaves in the pans to rise and went outside, facing the sunshine suddenly pouring in. Filled with praise for the trials that brought me to this place of awareness, I lifted prayers of sheer joy and began singing "It Is Well with My Soul." And it was.

Of course, dark times are an inescapable part of this world and trials still roll in, but I have finally learned to call on the peace of God's presence and the assurance of His steadfast love more quickly each time shadows threaten.

The ever-ready light of Christ that shines in brings songs of comfort to my lips and reminders of butterflies and bread.

Prayer for a Peace-Filled Life

Heavenly Father, I thank You for faith that carries me into the Light of Christ and for the peace that passes all understanding when I allow myself to feel heavenly arms of love wrapped around me. May I be a beacon of Your love with every step I take. In Jesus's holy name, Amen.

The Lord bless you and keep you; the Lord make his face shine on you and be gracious to you; the Lord turn his face toward you and give you peace.

Numbers 6:24–26 (NIV)

THE VISION

By Amanda Pennock

THE CAPTAIN OF THE PLANE made the announcement, "Ladies and gentlemen, we have started our final descent." I was in my preferred seat—the window, where I could look out into God's amazing creation. The flight had gone smoothly, and I was looking forward to landing and going to see my family.

As I was looking out the window, I noticed another plane rather close, descending at the same time. I watched as the runway came into view and our plane was getting closer and closer to the concrete. I prepared myself for the landing, when all at once, the plane accelerated and began ascending at a rapid speed. The captain made another announcement: "Ladies and gentlemen, we were not able to land due to traffic on the runway. We will circle around and try another approach. If we are still unable to land, we will have to try a different airport." The closest airport would be a two-hour drive down to my family. What about the rental car reservation I already had? I could have panicked, but I didn't. I was at perfect peace.

This was indeed a miracle. Just a few years ago, I would have been terrified and had a panic attack. Now, however, I felt God's presence and His perfect peace. I knew that everything would be all right. I just gave it all to God and knew He was in control. If we were to go to another airport, He had a reason for it. In the end, we were able to land after the second attempt and I was able to get my rental car and see my family on time.

• • •

I wasn't always at peace or willing to give it all to God. I was brought up in a home with an alcoholic father and a mother who was diagnosed with an anxiety disorder. She would have terrible panic attacks. She was unable to leave the house for years because her anxiety had become so problematic. By the time I was in my early twenties, I, too, had been diagnosed with an anxiety disorder. I also started suffering with panic attacks. I never knew when or where one would occur. For no apparent reason, I would be feeling fine one minute, and the next, I couldn't breathe.

I was twenty and standing in line at the bank with my two little girls the first time I remember having a panic attack. Out of nowhere, I felt faint and became very unsettled. It was as if I was paralyzed and couldn't move. Thank goodness, it only lasted a few minutes and then I was fine again. In the next few years, the attacks became more frequent. I had realized what was happening to me because I had watched my mom go through them and I was the one who had to talk her down each time.

My anxiety disorder caused me to be fearful of almost everything. One of my biggest fears was flying. The night before a flight, I would have nightmares. When I boarded the plane, I would grab the armrests, close my eyes tight, listen to my Christian praise and worship music, and pray during the entire flight. My stomach would be in knots, and I would be in physical pain. I absolutely hated to fly, but I sometimes lived so far from my family that I would need to fly in order to see them. My fear continued until one flight, when everything changed.

• • •

I was flying back home to Virginia after visiting my mom in Georgia. By now I was in my thirties and had been flying for about ten years. I felt even more increasingly nervous because I was alone and I was flying in the evening. My seat was in the back row of the plane. I started my ritual, grabbing the armrests and praying. Once we were in the air, we encountered turbulence. I started to panic. I prayed for God to help me, and He answered! At that moment, He gave me a vision of Him. He was a giant, and He was holding the plane in His hand as He walked across the earth. His peace filled me. When we continued to experience turbulence, I saw Him stepping over mountains. In an instant all the anxiety left.

Within a few months of this vision, my church was asking for volunteers to go on a mission trip to Bolivia. Never in my wildest dreams did I think I could fly on a plane that far, especially over the ocean. I really wanted to go. After all, God had done so much for me, and I wanted to give back. I decided to go—I knew He would be with me.

We all arrived very early at the airport to start our adventure to Bolivia. I must admit, I still had a nervous stomach and a small amount of anxiety. The flight was delayed for almost twelve hours, which caused even more anxiety. Despite that, I could feel God's peace. After an uneventful flight, during which I still prayed but didn't feel crippling anxiety, we arrived safely. That trip changed my life forever. I saw God in the eyes of the Bolivian people and was so grateful He was with me so I was able to go.

Complete freedom from my fear of flying didn't happen overnight. Every time I flew, I would pray and ask God to help me. Little by little the fear diminished. I was even able to start helping others who suffered with a fear of flying.

I also noticed a change in my everyday life. The panic attacks I had suffered for years stopped, so I no longer had to feel like I was in control. I also had more confidence. I understood that God's call for my life was to help others, and He was helping me to get to the place where I could fulfill it.

God has used me to bring supplies to people affected by hurricanes. I flew to Houston to help after Hurricane Harvey. I went on a mission trip to Puerto Rico to help a village there. I was able to fly back and forth from Virginia to Atlanta to help take care of my mom when she was dying of cancer.

Now I fly all over the world. I have been to all fifty states and several countries. I have been able to see so much of His creation and am eternally grateful. Only God would be able to change me like this, taking someone so consumed with anxiety and filling them with His perfect peace. That one vision did so much more than give me peace when I fly. It gives me peace every day because I know He is always with me, keeping me safe.

Prayer for a Peace-Filled Life

Father, thank You for always being there for me. When fear tries to come in, help me to remember that You hold me in the palm of Your hand and will never let me go.

A gentle answer turns away wrath, but a harsh word stirs up anger.

Proverbs 15:1 (NIV)

A SOFT ANSWER OPENED DOORS

By Bettie Boswell

TEACHING MUSIC at the elementary school level offered many adventures in acceptance and flexibility. Several schools provided a full classroom, but others weren't as obliging. During thirty-three years of teaching, I taught in many different types of rooms. Some schools provided a full classroom in the main building, while others used portable classrooms. In other situations, I shared rooms with other traveling teachers or used a portion of a room used primarily for storage.

Regardless of the size or location of the space, when class was in session, I wanted a place where my students could make a joyful noise, stomp their feet on the percussive floor, and play instruments without any outside interference. Of course, that wasn't always the case. In situations like former shop and science labs, I learned to accept the echoing sounds and had to encourage the use of quiet voices. When I shared rooms, I often found myself praying for peace over the constant rearranging of furniture and hunting for misplaced items. The smallest room I taught in was a gymnasium closet.

In that tiny gym closet, there was barely room to line three walls with enough kindergarten-sized chairs to seat a class. Any activities involving movement took place with a third of the class at a time. Those actions happened in a space with the dimensions of a good-sized pickup truck.

Being fairly new to the school system and thankful for that job, I made the best of the situation. I used the space to teach about pickup notes (not trucks!), rhythms, melodies, and simple instruments. Most of the time, the students and I sang or played without using the boom box, which sat a cabinet behind my shoulder. However, when my voice cracked or we needed to listen to a classic, like Beethoven, or move to folk dance arrangements, I made use of the device. On those occasions, music boomed into my classroom and vibrated through the wall behind me.

Most days, the tiny room on the other side of the wall stood empty. That closet's original purpose had probably been storage for the custodian's brooms. Due to space restraints in the packed school, it became a classroom for the speech therapist and her students. I had seen that teacher before, but we taught on separate schedules. We never had the need to connect until the sound of music blasted like a tidal wave through the wall between us.

With some students trying simple square dance moves and others clapping along, I almost missed the knocking at my door.

"Please turn the volume down. I'm trying to work with a student in my room behind this wall." The woman seemed pleasant, but I could tell she was not happy about the noise traveling through our shared wall.

My hand went to the volume control knob and I reduced the sound. At that moment I had a choice. Should I stand up for my rights as a teacher who needed to incorporate folk songs and dances in my curriculum or would I give in and eliminate the activity for the students who needed to move? Could we compromise somehow?

• • •

Choosing to walk in Jesus's footsteps, I opted for a peaceful resolution that would hopefully satisfy everyone. I promised to keep the volume down while continuing with the required activity. During my break, I rearranged furniture and placed the offending boom box in a far corner of the tiny music room. In the following days, my students learned to clap with two fingers instead of a full hand. I also visited my neighbor and invited her to chat about improvements if my changes weren't helping.

Placing the sound machine in a different corner of the room worked wonders. Vibrations no longer traveled through the wall, distracting speech students from their tutoring. My music classes continued to meet the standards, and students learned to control their noise level—most of the time. And I made a new friend who needed someone to chat with.

The speech therapist moved from building to building within the district, so she didn't have many opportunities for friendly conversations. She was also a single woman who lived alone. Our initial chitchat turned into conversations about our respective positions, students, her cat, and music. Our friendship grew as she watched my students perform a musical I had written. She expressed a desire to join me in that type of endeavor, and we worked together to complete a couple of musicals for student performances. Our friendship blossomed as we spent more time together and discovered common interests.

As with any relationship, ours required some give-and-take. We both had ideas about what we wanted for our musicals. I gave in many times, seeking to keep the peace, which didn't always give me serenity. Though we continued to be friends, I eventually returned to making musicals on my own, until a call to create brought us back together.

During one of our conversations outside our small classrooms, I mentioned that the director of the local historical museum had asked about the composition of a dedication song for one of their new acquisitions—a train depot that had been relocated onto their property. Of course, my friend wanted to be involved. We both met with the curator to gather information about the history of trains in the area.

My friend called a couple of days later with the news that she had written lyrics for several songs. She wanted to approach the curator with the idea of a community theater production about our area. The curator loved the idea, so we began writing a script together.

This time I wasn't afraid to argue my points as we wrote. I realized I needed to be at peace with myself while being at peace with the Lord. I requested that there be no profanity in the production and was able to change my friend's mind when the issue arose. God did His part too. We wrote about a historic figure coming to town, thinking him being there was impossible, other than in the world of fiction. But when I researched the man, there was evidence he'd actually been in a nearby village on the date we chose for our setting. He might have even passed through our town on the train we were writing about. There were several other God moments, but that one stands out in my memory.

• • •

With the support of the community, the musical became a reality. During production, I often acted as a peacemaker between my friend's strong persona and the directing staff. Our relationship had grown to the point where I understood her personality. That knowledge came in handy when smoothing over misunderstandings and frustrations. After a successful run of the play, we agreed to be friends, but not create together. Our friendship continues to this day.

My friend's concern for her students and our mutual love of music led us to create several musicals during our teaching years. Those events would never have occurred if

I had answered her initial complaints about my boom box in a way that stirred up wrath instead of looking for peace. I am thankful God gave me the wisdom to make a choice pleasing to Him.

Prayer for a Peace-Filled Life

Dear Lord, when I have a choice between answering in anger or offering a calming solution, please give me strength to wisely choose Your peace. In Jesus's name, Amen.

For Christ did not send me to baptize, but to preach the gospel—not with wisdom and eloquence, lest the cross of Christ be emptied of its power.

1 Corinthians 1:17 (NIV)

ACCORDING TO THE BARNA GROUP, a research and resource group, 70 percent of Christians walk away from their faith in college. Sadly, most don't return to God even after graduation. It's with good reason that parents worry about their kids when they go off to university. Last fall, I found myself in the same boat when we moved our oldest son, Zack, into his dorm. All I could do was trust and pray. I had no idea that Zack joining the rugby team would be the answer to those prayers.

Pre-COVID, the team had the worst reputation on campus for extreme misbehavior, even to the point of charges being filed against one player for sexual assault. Post-COVID, the players vowed to change that. Smitty was the most influential in that process, despite being rough around the edges and one of the biggest partiers in the group.

All thirty players were required to eat dinner together in the cafeteria each night. Subtly and silently, Smitty would bow his head and pray before he ate. Because he was one of the "cool" guys the other players looked up to, it didn't take long for his teammates to notice. One by one, each joined him in prayer. Before long, the entire team was praying together before meals and before every game they played. The curiosity didn't end there. It led Jeremy, another player, to read his Bible daily, resulting in his baptism and a full entry into the faith. It also led my Zack to read his Bible every night before bed, leading him to form his own personal relationship with Christ that grows stronger by the day. Several other teammates who had never been exposed to faith are taking their own baby steps in their personal journeys.

Smitty isn't well spoken, nor a star student or player. He simply lives out his conviction that Jesus is The Way, and he does so with courage, changing the trajectory of several college students' lives in the process.

People like Smitty are everywhere, stepping out in faith and touching lives. They don't need to be eloquent or overbearing in their evangelization. They just need to believe in the power of the cross, have the courage to live out its message, and let God do the rest. When they do, they bring joy and peace to so many, as well as to the families who love them.

—Claire McGarry

Whatever you have learned or received or heard from me, or seen in me—put it into practice. And the God of peace will be with you.

Philippians 4:9 (NIV)

A STRANGER'S PRAYER

By Kristy Dewberry

I WAS ALWAYS GLAD to see Dad's number on my caller ID. We shared the same sense of humor and personality traits. He wasn't just my father—he was also my friend.

"Hey, Dad."

"Honey, could you look up pancreatic cancer on the computer?" he asked.

With those ten words our lives were about to change. I knew nothing about pancreatic cancer. I just knew that all cancer was bad, but with proper treatment people could live a long time. I personally knew a couple of women who had survived breast cancer. I typed in "pancreatic cancer," already planning my upbeat speech. He would beat this.

I hit the enter button. Bad news bombarded me, with "low survival rate" being the common theme.

How do I repeat those ugly words aloud to my father, much less over the phone? Many people feel like their heart stops when they receive bad news, but mine began pumping harder than ever. I couldn't lie, but maybe I could find a glimmer of hope to soften my news.

"If it's caught early, or if it's at an early stage, then that can increase the survival rate," I said.

If anything, my effort at finding positive news backfired. Dad's oncologist had already advised him that he was at a later stage and that he had six months or less to live.

• • •

Back then, in 2007, there were fewer treatment options than there are now. As a last resort, the oncologist referred Dad to a surgeon for a Whipple procedure, a surgery to remove the tumors from the head of the pancreas. If it was successful, it might buy Dad more time. The surgeon had warned us that the odds weren't in Dad's favor, but despite that, I had pinned all my hopes and prayers on this surgery, praying that God would bless it to extend Dad's life.

When the surgeon met our family in the waiting room, he bluntly informed us that the surgery didn't work. The pancreatic cancer was attached to vital organs and he couldn't get to it.

I burst into tears.

The surgeon reacted defensively.

"Why are you surprised? I told you it probably wouldn't work," he snapped. "He'll be in the recovery room. A nurse will let you know when you can go in there." Without giving us time for any questions, he headed to his next surgery.

My husband, Don, put his arms around me and led me to the empty chapel.

"Why didn't God answer my prayer? Why would Dad's life be cut short? He's been planning his retirement for years. I thought that the surgery would work and that Dad would see it as a miracle. He'd finally realize that he wanted a relationship with God."

Somehow, despite not being raised in a godly home, my two sisters and I were believers. We still hoped our parents would become believers as well.

"We can go in the recovery room now," my sister, Karen, said from the chapel door. "Dad's about to wake up."

Dad opened his eyes to see the tearful expressions of my sisters and me.

"It didn't work, did it?"

There was no need to answer.

We all crowded into an elevator with Dad and an orderly who was pushing the wheeled stretcher. We were headed to his assigned hospital room, where he could recuperate. As the elevator doors closed, I noticed a man in the back corner, behind me. I wondered how I'd missed seeing him when I first stepped in.

"Hi," I said and smiled weakly. I knew my eyes must be swollen and red.

His eyes, on the other hand, were full of compassion and empathy.

He nodded toward Dad.

"Your father must be well loved," he said.

My eyes filled with tears yet again.

"He is."

"I'm going to pray for him and your family." He lightly touched my arm with his hand. I felt warmth through my sleeve, and somehow his simple touch communicated hope and peace.

The elevator doors opened and I followed my family out. When I turned around to thank the stranger, he was gone.

"What a nice man," I said to the others. "I'm glad he's going to pray for us."

"Who?" My sister asked.

"The man in the elevator," I said. Who else would I be talking about?

They looked at me blankly, then turned away.

• • •

Dad recuperated, and once he got home, he began walking a couple of miles a day and planning a trip. He wanted to cram as much living as possible into the next two to six months. Mom, with her Alzheimer's, didn't handle stress well, but she did her best to make us feel welcome, as our whole family rallied around him.

Our family was suddenly spending more time together than ever. Every morning when I prayed, I gave thanks to God for the extra time he provided for us to be with Dad. Occasionally, though, on the harder days, I'd feel discouraged, hopeless. On those days, God would bring to mind the man in the elevator, who'd promised to pray for us. At first, I thought of him as "the elevator man," but later, as I remembered the feeling of peace I received when he touched my arm, I began to think of him as my angel of peace.

Six months later, Dad was still going strong. He and Mom went to Anna Maria, Florida, for two months, and my sisters and I, along with our spouses, took turns visiting them for a week at a time. As Dad and I walked the beach every morning, I'd accumulate unusual shells and special memories.

The following year, Dad took us on a Thanksgiving cruise. We ate turkey and dressing on the ship. We had plenty to be thankful for that year.

We went to Branson, Missouri, to see Silver Dollar City's Christmas decorations and enjoy the Christmas music and hot chocolate.

The third year, we traveled by train from Oklahoma City to Fort Worth, Texas, where we went to Billie Bob's to enjoy country music and then walked around Cowtown. We laughed as we took pictures of Mom and Dad sitting on a bull.

The fourth year, we planned a fiftieth wedding anniversary celebration.

Throughout the years and in between our vacations together, we visited Mom and Dad at their lake trailer, took Dad to movies and out to dinner, and rooted for the Oklahoma University Sooners. Dad even had the strength to help me attempt to plant a garden.

Dad's oncologist began referring to him as Superman and using his case to encourage his other patients. We were too busy living to think much about dying, although I'd be lying if I said it wasn't lurking in the back of my mind. But when fear tried to take hold of me, especially during the nighttime, I'd remember the stranger's touch and the feeling of peace it provided, and I'd rest easy.

• • •

Sometime during the fourth year, Karen's pastor visited Dad. Dad took a liking to Pastor Tom and looked forward to his visits. Pastor Tom was not one to push people to God. He just told them frankly what God meant to him and let them form their own opinion. Dad told Pastor Tom that he wanted a relationship with God before he died, but he felt guilty, as if he were acting like a last-minute quarterback. Pastor Tom told him it was better to join the game at the end than to have never played at all.

More time passed and Dad's faith grew.

"Would you baptize me, Pastor?" he asked.

It turned out that Mom wanted to be included, and I like to believe that despite her Alzheimer's, God was involved in her change of heart as well. After the baptism, Dad began slowing down. Don and I visited my parents at their lake trailer and I could tell Dad was in more pain than usual, although he tried to hide it. He finally admitted that he needed medical help, so we rushed him to the hospital.

Soon after, the oncologist gave us the bad news. He had a blockage in his stomach and could no longer eat food. He could try to put Dad on a feeding machine that might prolong his life for a short period. Dad looked at me, and asked, "What should I do?"

I consider myself a strong female, but no daughter wants to make a decision like that for her dad. I choked back tears.

"I can't make that decision. Obviously, I want you around for as long as possible, but you need to make the choice that's best for you."

He chose to try it, but it wasn't successful. Although Dad's life on earth was going to end, thanks to the extra time God gave Dad to come to Him, his eternal heavenly life would continue.

Randy, our hospice worker, joined our family to guide us through Dad's final days on earth. Dad refused pain medications. He wanted his mind clear for as long as he was alive. We stayed around the clock, playing his favorite songs and watching old tapes of Johnny Carson shows. Dad asked me to have them play "Softly and Tenderly" at his funeral.

He closed his eyes at one point and looked exhausted. I went to his side and held his hand in mine. "If you feel God's presence or an angel beckoning to you, it's OK to go. We'll be fine." He took one last breath and he was gone. My sister and nephew speak to this day of how they felt a heavenly spirt in the room come to take Dad home. As for me, I felt a warm touch on my arm of love, compassion . . . and peace.

Prayer for a Peace-Filled Life

Father, sometimes I struggle to find peace in the midst of a difficult situation. Help me to allow Your peace to guard my heart and mind from feelings of fear and hopelessness, despite the circumstances surrounding me.

Strive for peace with everyone, and for the holiness without which no one will see the Lord.

Hebrews 12:14 (ESV)

THE EXTENDED HAND

By Claire McGarry

BACK IN THE EARLY 1990s, I spent three years as a missionary in Guatemala. My intention was to give my time and energy in Jesus's name to somehow make people's lives better. No matter how hard I tried to achieve that goal, though, I'm certain my life was impacted more than the lives of the people I served. It didn't happen during deep and profound movie moments, with a defined before and after. Instead, it was in all the small ways I witnessed Jesus in the Guatemalan people and how freely they gave of their hearts.

One such moment happened on a day I took a chicken bus, a standard mode of transportation in Guatemala. These brightly colored buses carry not only locals and tourists but also sometimes produce, pets, and chickens, thus the name. I was on my way back from a neighboring town where

I'd gone to attend church services. It was a usual Sunday, nothing out of the ordinary, except I had the bench seat on the old school bus all to myself. But not for long. As we stopped at the army barracks, a small girl of about ten got on and sat beside me. Actually, I should say she sat almost on top of me. Thinking a third person would join us, she moved over right next to me. The third person never sat down, but in her innocence, she stayed put. We began to chat in Spanish. I quickly learned her name was Yolanda.

As the bus rolled along, I couldn't help but be moved by her. After all, her small body leaned up against my whole left side as she fit perfectly into the space behind my arm. Yet, something else about Yolanda touched my heart. In that moment, I couldn't put my finger on why. She wasn't a beautiful child. She had warts all over the backs of her hands. And although her dress was clean, the fabric was torn and faded, and pulled at the seams where it was too small. Regardless, she held herself with grace and was simplicity embodied.

She was holding an ear of corn, a typical snack in Guatemala, and was nibbling on it. On impulse, I offered her some of the nachos I was eating. A twinkle came into her eyes and a self-conscious giggle spilled from her lips, telling me she wasn't accustomed to people giving her things. Nonetheless, she opened her hand, received the chips, and thanked me. Before she ate even one nacho, she plucked corn kernel after corn kernel from the cob she was eating. When her hand could hold no more, she extended it to me. I smiled and accepted the corn graciously, moved she would share what little she had.

When I looked down again, she was extending her nacho-filled hand to the woman across the aisle. I was a bit sad, afraid she didn't like my gift. So, I asked her. She said she liked nachos, but wanted to share with her mother. Her completely selfless act prompted me to reach into my bag again and give her more. Once again, she picked more corn kernels from her cob to give to me before she ate even a single chip.

• • •

Back and forth we went, exchanging chips and corn, until my bag was as empty as her plucked cob. "*Terminamos,*" I said ("we ran out"), as I placed the plastic bag in my backpack. "*Sí,*" she answered, as she tossed her cob out the bus window. I smiled to myself, grateful it wasn't the reverse: the empty cob in my backpack and the plastic bag out the window!

She went on to tell me that she and her mother visited her brother at the army barracks every Sunday, and occasionally during the week, "*si Dios lo permite*" ("God willing"). She said they lived over two hours away by bus. From her face, though, I could see she viewed the trip as an adventure.

Then I let her use my Walkman. I showed her what all the buttons were for and apologized because the music was in English, not Spanish. With pride, she let me put the earphones on her head. She constantly looked around to be sure others noticed what she had. Yet, never once did she ask me if she could keep my Walkman, like so many others had when I'd let them try it. It seemed there wasn't a jealous or greedy bone in her little body. She was just as happy to give it back to me when she was done as she had been to use it.

I continued struggling to figure out why her mere presence was giving me so much. Her little body tucked behind mine and those hands with their warts giving me the corn were churning up so many emotions. The more I reflected, the more I could name gratitude, connection, joy, and admiration. Here was a child who had so little, yet was giving me everything she had: her corn, her time, and her affection. I could tell it never occurred to her to put a limit on any of them. She seemed to accept her place in the world, knowing she was a child of God, perfectly made, despite her warts. Consequently, peace exuded from her, along with joy.

Suddenly, I recalled the verses in Matthew 18. When Jesus was asked who was the greatest in the kingdom of Heaven, He called over a little child. Yolanda herself could have been that very child Jesus held up as the example of pure faith and humility we should all emulate. I felt as if He were doing it in that moment just for me: teaching me how to live, how to treat others, how to truly make the world a better place.

• • •

As my heart expanded with all that Yolanda was giving me, I wanted to return the favor. I kept thinking about the other unopened bag of nachos in my backpack. I imagined placing the full bag in her hands before I got off the bus. I also imagined her grateful eyes shining up at me—eyes that would emblazon my face on her heart forever, so much so that she would tell her friends, "Oh, I met this wonderful American woman on a bus once . . ." and proceed to say nice things about me. With the lessons she was teaching me still fresh in my mind, I recognized the opportunity to put them into practice right there and then.

That's why I decided to leave the nachos where they were when I got to my stop. Yes, Yolanda and I had been exchanging "things" that day, but we shared much more than that. This little girl had taught me that giving takes on a whole new meaning when it's done without pretense and with pure intention. Our exchange hadn't been about the food we'd given to each other. It had been about two people, from completely different worlds, sharing from the heart, making the moment holy.

As I stood to get off at my stop, I gave her my heart through my eyes as I said, *"Vaya con Dios!"* ("Go with God").

Prayer for a Peace-Filled Life

God of True Tranquility, keep us open to the peace You give us through the hearts of others. Amen.

Listen to me, all who hope for deliverance—all who seek the LORD! Consider the rock from which you were cut, the quarry from which you were mined.

Isaiah 51:1 (NLT)

THE ROOTS OF A STRONG TREE

By Laurie Thurneck

DAD, NOW ELDERLY, recently faced a health crisis that could become serious, and Mom was getting older too. They were courageous, but I didn't manage the uncertainty as well. *Where would home be without Mom and Dad?*

For most of my life, when people asked me where I was from, I didn't know what to say. We had moved often and crisscrossed the country several times before I was fourteen, when we settled in Virginia. Dad was in the air force and worked in the space program from the California coast, where I was born. Mom said that when I heard a missile launch, I would toddle outside, exclaiming proudly to the neighborhood,

"That's my Dad's rocket." Wherever we moved, and even when I left good friends behind, my family was with me, and home was wherever we were. My family felt more like home than a place ever had.

Not knowing how to answer that simple question of where I was from was suddenly more serious at the thought of losing my parents, especially because I had never married and had my own children. I felt like the real-life "Old Maid" from the card game that we used to play with our grandmother. Grandma would always take the dreaded card if we placed it up high above the others in our hands.

Now, at middle age, I found myself reviewing my life, some might call it a midlife crisis. I felt sorrow over mistakes I had made and wished the impossible—that I could have a do-over. I would make better choices. My deepest regret was not having children. My sisters had husbands and children, and I compared myself to them. I wondered who would be by my side when I got old. The thought of losing my parents leveled me, and even praying and reading my Bible didn't bring the comfort that it usually did. My doctor diagnosed me with anxious depression.

• • •

Dad was always my trusted adviser, so I turned to him. I wanted to support him and also soothe my own anxiety. When Dad was middle-aged, he had worked on our family tree. He did it the old-fashioned way, going to cemeteries, writing away for records, and looking in family Bibles.

A friend had told me about the website Ancestry.com, so I signed up and asked Dad to help. I felt the pain of deep regret that my tree wouldn't grow branches but wanted an activity to keep me close to Dad.

"Why don't we start with Mom's side? They've been here a long time," he said. We had no idea how long! On my summer break from teaching school, we set up our computers and worked at the same sturdy oak table that he had built model airplanes on as a boy. We were surprised to find several Baptist ministers. The first left the Philadelphia area as a missionary to go west before the American Revolution. His travels led him to establish his church near Leesburg, Virginia. "He didn't get very far west," I commented. Dad said that "going out west" back then meant crossing over the Blue Ridge Mountains. We laughed about that for a while, and I was reminded of trips I had taken to Leesburg for my dog to see an eye specialist. I wished I had known of the church then as Reverend Marks, my sixth great-grandfather, is buried in the cemetery there.

The Reverend was said to have been a chaplain in George Washington's army. I think of his story now when I look at the print in my parents' living room of George Washington kneeling in prayer beside his white horse. The Reverend's son, my fifth great-grandfather, was also a Revolutionary War veteran. Their courage and sacrifice for our freedoms give new meaning to the print, and I have a deeper appreciation for my country.

The Reverend's granddaughter, my fourth great-grandmother, would marry another Baptist minister.

Their daughter, my third great-grandmother, married yet another. *Wow! I had come from people of faith, like me.* I told Dad that I thought Grandpa may have missed his calling. "He prayed fervently," Dad reminded me. Grandpa's prayer from the recesses of my memory came back to me: "Heavenly Father, we thank Thee, for these blessings that we are about to receive," his solemn prayer before every meal. I wondered how many generations back that prayer went.

Sometimes wills popped up in our searches, and that was like finding gold. That's where we found the human connection, the record of love and careful concern and care. The first Reverend arranged for firewood, already cut, to be delivered to his wife's front door after his death. He wanted her to be warm, and that warmed my heart. Occasionally, animals were mentioned, including horses with evocative names like Highstepper.

• • •

As we worked over several years, mostly during the summers, when I wasn't teaching, Dad bravely went through three surgeries. Ever my inspiration, his faith never wavered, and he stayed cheerful. His example taught me how to face the same human fear surely everyone in our tree had, of illness and growing old.

We sat at the table or shared our discoveries over the phone, and hints to our ancestors in Virginia kept popping up until they crowded our computer screens. Those from Grandma's side were also in Virginia in prerevolutionary years. I was filled with awe that they were spread out around me like the roots of a tree, my tree. Some lived in Swift Run Gap, near where I taught my dual-enrollment students in Greene County. On the scenic drive to teach, I would imagine my forebears' home in the Blue Ridge Mountains. Another helped settle the Shenandoah Valley, just over Afton Mountain and a short drive away. The nearby mountains began to ground me in the knowledge that my ancestors lived near me and are part of me. Their lives touched me.

Thankfully, we didn't lose Dad. He is now free of the illness that threatened him, and over time, feelings of gratitude replaced my depression. Each new discovery in our tree was a revelation that pushed my anxieties aside. I found comfort in being part of something bigger that, for me, went backward instead of forward. I know where I'm from and feel at peace in it. I'm home. Who but God could have known?

Prayer for a Peace-Filled Life

Heavenly Father, thank You for my family and home. When I'm afraid, help me to remember that You know me and know my place in the world even when I can't fathom how I fit. Your goodness fills me with peace. In Jesus's name, Amen.

Where, O death, is your victory? Where, O death, is your sting? But thanks be to God! He gives us the victory through our Lord Jesus Christ.

1 Corinthians 15:55, 57 (NIV)

BUILT ON TRUST

By Anne Watson

THROUGHOUT MY YEARS as a Christian, I never gave much thought to trust. Time and again, the Bible gives the command to trust in the Lord with my whole being. Since I know God's best waits on the other side of obedience, it was not difficult to trust Him. And the bonus? The realization that this command to trust often includes a promise from God.

• • •

In the process of moving from California to Oregon after my husband retired, he and I were looking for an opportunity to buy property and build our dream house. The real estate agent took us to various sites, but none fit into our vision of the place for our forever home. After several days of searching, discouragement crept in. Nothing we saw met our criteria.

Amazingly, without realizing it, our agent had saved the best for last—20 acres sitting high on a hill overlooking the beautiful, lush Applegate Valley. This location was God's answer to our prayers, and it was easy saying yes to Him. We had a fixed budget for the entire project—property and construction—and we were determined not to deviate from it. We were on a fast track for finding property and the broker told us this one would go quickly, so we made an offer commensurate with our budget. The seller, however, was adamant he would not budge on the price and rejected our offer, expecting a counteroffer for his land.

Leery of building a house on the side of a mountain, we decided to continue the due diligence process by visiting the county planning offices to request information for the plethora of questions my detail-oriented husband needed answers for. The land management staff suggested we contact a civil engineer to go out and look at the property. While my husband was on hold with the engineer's office, I went to use the facilities.

Alone in the ladies' room, I heard what can only be described as the closest thing I'd ever experienced to hearing God's voice. He asked, "Do you trust Me?"

Flustered, I anxiously looked around to see who had spoken to me. When I sensed it was God speaking to my spirit, I said, "Yes, Lord, I trust You."

"Do you *really* trust Me?"

"Yes, Lord, I *really* trust You."

The message was loud and clear. I felt as if God would have us put an end to the due diligence for the twenty-acre parcel.

When I walked out of the ladies' room, my husband was pacing in the outer corridor of the planning department with his cell phone to his ear, his call still on hold. I could see the stress on his face. I grasped both his shoulders, looked him in the eyes, and said, "We need to stop this process." The overwhelming relief on his face caused me to realize I needed to listen to God to trust Him, which meant letting go of this property. He closed his eyes, took a deep breath, and whispered, "Thank God."

Even though I valiantly attempted to hide my feelings when we shared the news with our agent, disheartened tears flowed. This seemed strange because trusting God was how I lived my life, and He obviously knew something about that property we did not. Unfortunately, telling myself I could sacrifice my dream for my husband's peace of mind did little to squelch the disappointment. We ultimately came away believing God had something better for us.

• • •

Not many weeks later, we received a call from our agent with the exciting news that the seller had decided to accept our offer. For some unknown reason, my husband was ready to jump on the deal. When I reminded him that he had, not long ago, made clear his uncertainty with regard to the safety of building with a mountain mere feet from the back of our proposed house site, he said he felt confident we could figure out a plan that would work. Who was I to argue against the reality of building my dream house? Needless to say, I shouted my profound thankfulness to God from the top of the mountain, "Yes, Lord, I definitely trust You."

Throughout the building process and on into our time living in our beautiful home, the other question God had asked me—"Do you *really* trust Me?"—never came to mind. Originally, I thought the question might be a test from God. Was my faith really as solid as I thought it was? I guess you could say the profusion of trials that go with building a house were somehow in the back of my mind as the answer.

Less than two years later, though, it became apparent that my concept of the answer to that question was as far from God's meaning as it could be, when Jesus graciously escorted my husband to heaven, after a short—exactly one month from the day of diagnosis—bout with cancer.

Devastation didn't begin to express my emotions. More like terror. My purpose for living gone. My security crumbled. Future? Nonexistent without my husband.

Sitting alone on the top step of our two-story *dream* home, slumped against the railing, I clutched my husband's leather jacket to my chest and wailed. Never before had I cried so hard or felt such excruciating pain. I remember shouting, "Lord, I can't do this. I *cannot* do this!"

Memories swamped my heart and caused the sobbing to intensify.

I will never hear his voice again or laugh with him or feel the warmth of his strong arms around me. Lord, what were You thinking?

Without warning, my shivering ceased, the sobbing turned into quick short breaths, and it felt like a warm quilt was being wrapped around my shoulders. God's presence became palpable.

Reading about the Father's incomprehensible peace was one thing, but actually experiencing it was another. The unbearable pain drained from me. A supernatural warmth enveloped me. Nothing else mattered except the loving presence of Jesus. My Comforter, the Holy Spirit, whispered to my spirit, "I will never leave you."

I closed my eyes, breathed deep, and felt as if all my senses were on high alert. Smiling, I simply said, "Yes, Lord, I *really* trust You."

• • •

There has been a huge learning curve in my life. Throughout the days, months, and years since my husband's homegoing, not only did I struggle to take on the myriad responsibilities he had handled with ease, but I also experienced the reality that I truly can do all things through Christ who strengthens me. In this new season, I am growing up. Emotionally. Mentally. Physically. Definitely spiritually.

Has it been easy? No. Do I trust God in the midst of this major life change? Absolutely. After all, He is the one who spoke to me in the ladies' room long ago when I was searching for an answer about buying the mountainside property for our dream home. Perhaps I needed to understand what God was really asking me then—to trust Him—in order to learn how to now lean on Him completely. To slow down and receive the peace that inhabits the splendor of His presence and enjoy the glory of His creation.

More than anything, I cling to the hope, the reality, that heaven awaits all who belong to Jesus.

Prayer for a Peace-Filled Life

Lord, You prove Yourself trustworthy in every detail of my life. I need only to take the time to watch and listen to experience Your faithfulness. Give me spiritual eyes to see and ears to hear. Don't let me miss You in the midst of the difficult.

For we are God's handiwork, created in Christ Jesus to do good works, which God prepared in advance for us to do.

Ephesians 2:10 (NIV)

SOME OF US are blessed with 20/20 vision, but even that isn't enough to see things the way God does. Throw in our earthly inclination to judge or complain too quickly and we're prone to label something that brings us pain or discomfort as "bad." Rather than relying on God's promise that He will work for our good no matter the circumstance, we remain swallowed up by our own suffering, letting it convince us we've been abandoned by God.

My friend Julie and her husband, Steve, could have gone the route of lamenting their suffering after Steve's skiing accident. It was their faith that had them choosing a different perspective.

One day, when Steve was speeding down the ski slopes, he hit two unexpected moguls in the terrain that launched him 30 feet into the air. The six broken ribs and punctured lung were an incredible blow to the fifty-five-year-old father of five who was the sole provider through his auto-repair business. The bad news didn't end there, though. The CT scan also showed an enlarged aortic aneurysm. Further tests showed that Steve had it well before the skiing accident. Had he not broken his ribs and needed the CT scan, the aneurysm would have gone undetected and killed him instantly when it finally burst. After undergoing open-heart surgery to remove the aneurysm and replace the aortic valve, Steve is now fine. Both he and Julie recognize the gift they were given. They now praise God for broken ribs.

It's not always easy to see how one hardship helps us avoid another. Stories like Steve's remind us to stand on God's promise of always working for the good of those who love Him. Joseph did when his brothers sold him into slavery, only to then save them, and all of Egypt, from famine (Genesis 41). Ruth did when she vowed to follow Naomi to Judah, widowed and penniless, only to marry Boaz, give birth to Obed, and become the great-grandmother of David, the eventual king of Israel (Ruth 1:16–4:17).

Our stories may not have such dramatic twists, but when we love God and praise Him according to His will, we can trust that He is working for our good. Doing so gives purpose to our hardships and our pain.

—Claire McGarry

Jesus came and stood among them and said, "Peace be with you!" After he said this, he showed them his hands and side.

John 20:19–20 (NIV)

FINDING PEACE IN THE WOUNDS

By Heather Jepsen

I HAVE NEVER BEEN a brave person. I can't watch scary movies, and I don't go to theme parks and ride roller coasters. I am more of a stay-at-home-and-take-it-easy kind of girl. A cup of tea and a nice book to read are my perfect afternoon friends. I do my best to avoid things I think are fearful.

One thing I find frightening that I can't avoid is surgery. I remember once when I was in my twenties and I needed to have oral surgery. As the nurse brought me in to the surgical area I was overcome with fear. I started yelling, "I'm scared, I'm scared, I'm scared," and I couldn't stop. Even though I knew I was acting impolitely, I couldn't help myself. I was so terribly afraid of what was about to happen that all I could do was cry out. Hurriedly the nurse got an IV inserted and quickly filled me with anesthesia so I would fall asleep. Later on, I woke up and I was fine, but I was so embarrassed about letting my fear get the better of me.

• • •

Twenty years later, when I was in my late forties, I was diagnosed with a rare condition called giant cell tumor. This is an aggressive but noncancerous tumor that often grows in the fluid around joints. My tumor was growing in the fluid around the tendon in my left ankle. And it was huge. The only cure for this disease is to try to cut the tumor out.

So back into surgery I went, but this time I was older and wiser. Instead of an oral surgeon's office setting, this was a real hospital affair. Nervously I sat and waited for my time to come.

If you have ever been to a hospital for a scheduled surgery, then you know what this is like. You have plenty of time to sit in the pre-op area and stew in your anxiety. People come and people go. The surgeon visits and the nurses get you ready. But mostly you just sit there and wait. This is the time when fear begins to grow, a slight gnawing away in the belly. I tried to encourage myself to relax. God was with me; I could do this.

When the time for my surgery arrived, everything suddenly happened in a rush. A different crew of nurses came and hurriedly wheeled me out of pre-op and down a hall into the surgical room. That is when my fear spiked. Something about their rushing and my impending sense of pain really got me going. I was able not to cry out this time. Instead, I muttered a prayer under my breath, "God be with me . . . God be with me . . . God be with me." The surgical room was so bright and so cold and so very scary. The surgical table was so small, and I felt so afraid and vulnerable. I lay down and right away the mask was over my nose and mouth. Three deep breaths and I was asleep.

When I woke up, it was into a fog of pain. My ankle and leg were so sore, but the doctor thought he got all the tumor, so that was good news. When it was all over, I had a huge scar and it would be six months before I could walk normally again.

The following spring, just as I was confidently on my feet again without a cane, Easter arrived. I am a pastor, so this is my busy season. As I was working my way through the scriptures of the season, I was struck by the ending of the gospel of John. When the risen Christ appears to the disciples, He shows them His wounds. He offers peace, but it is a peace that comes from a place of woundedness. He has scars in His hands and side. Jesus takes the time to show the disciples that He knows suffering and fear. Reading these texts anew with my own fresh 15-inch scar was transformative. Like Jesus, I have deep wounds, and I realized I could use that place of suffering and pain as a means of offering peace to others.

• • •

Unfortunately, the following summer my tumor returned, which is not uncommon for the disease. I was so certain that one surgery would be enough, but that was not to be the case.

At this point in my journey with giant cell tumor, I have undergone four surgeries in the same location, as well as a removal of tendons from my thigh to replace the ones the tumor destroyed in my ankle. Lots of surgeries, more scarring, and many long months of recovery are the pattern of my life now.

I wish I could say that I am no longer afraid when I go into surgery, but I still am. I still always pray as I am wheeled into the surgical room, "God be with me . . . God be with me." But I have found peace with the process as it becomes more familiar. I expect the sudden sense of rushing that will spike my anxiety. I know that the room will be bright and cold, the bed will be small, and I will be afraid. I think my body knows it is going to get hurt and so some of my fear response is out of my control. I just try to keep my worried mind in check.

My greater struggle is with the recovery process. I have spent years in a cycle of surgery followed by long recovery as I learn to walk again. I have had to adjust to chronic pain and no sensation at all in the bottom of my foot.

More than ever, I struggle mentally in the weeks and months after each surgery. How can I keep going? How can I keep my spirits up if this is to be the pattern of my life? I often think I am just prolonging the inevitable—an amputation of my foot. But my doctor always insists we have one more chance. Each time we find the tumor anew, he wants one more try to excise the tumor and save my foot, no matter the suffering that follows.

In all my struggles, I have found a deep sense of peace by thinking back to the wounded Christ. Jesus doesn't come back from resurrection healed and whole. Instead, He still bears the scars of His trauma. I bear the scars of my trauma and pain, and these lessons help me to be a better pastor. Jesus shows His wounds and then offers the disciples peace. Peace amid the signs of suffering. That is the story I hold on to now. Every step I take with my left foot is a reminder of the peace offered by the wounded Christ.

I think the reason I fear surgery so much is the sense of being out of control. Just like scary movies and roller-coaster rides, I don't like not knowing what is going to happen next. I don't like being out of control of my body or my situation. But that's exactly what faith is, isn't it? Faith is trusting in God to take control, to keep us safe, to hold us in His hands and power during difficult moments of our lives. Faith is praying "God be with me" and having the trust that God really will be with me. Usually, we don't have to put this to the test, but when we are facing things that cause us fear, then we come face-to-face with the depth of our faith.

The wounded Christ knows suffering and pain, and yet He has conquered all. I look to Christ when I face my own periods of suffering and pain. And in my moments of greatest fear, I rely on Christ to bring me peace.

Prayer for a Peace-Filled Life

Dear Jesus, when I am afraid, help me to trust in Your peace. I lean on You in faith, and You comfort my worried heart. God, be with me. Amen.

You will keep in perfect peace all who trust in you, all whose thoughts are fixed on you!

Isaiah 26:3 (NLT)

A DIMPLE AND THE DAY I LEARNED TO TRUST

By Laurie Davies

"ISN'T THAT A CUTE DIMPLE?" I asked my three-month-old son's pediatrician, as she examined his lower back during a routine checkup. After a rough-and-tumble entrance into the world with a tube down his throat and a short stint in the neonatal intensive care unit, he had rebounded quickly from an airway blockage at birth. Easygoing, and a great eater and sleeper, my son was a happy baby. Lately he'd been all smiles.

The doctor frowned.

Quickly unclipping a medical penlight from her coat, she shone it directly onto—and then into—the dimple.

She jotted a note on his chart as my son cooed and grasped for her stethoscope.

"I can't see a point where this closes," she said, clicking the penlight off and pointing her attention to me.

"What does that mean?" I tried to sound calm. Suddenly, the dimple in my baby's lower back didn't seem cute.

"It can mean spina bifida, something less serious, or nothing at all. It might be closed and I just can't see it with my eye. It's called a sacral dimple, and if it is open into the spinal canal, infection can be serious," she said, scrawling out an immediate order for an MRI and instructing her assistant to schedule it for me as a priority scan.

• • •

Diaper changes, once just a gross rite of passage into parenthood, now became full-scale sanitary matters of great importance. My husband and I moved in to change our son's diaper if we perceived even a hint of activity.

We woke every hour through the night to check on him. We'd waited quite a few years for this little guy and we couldn't bear the thought of bacteria traveling through that dimple into his spinal cord, causing an infection that could lead to anything from nerve damage and weakness in his legs to lifelong—or life-shortening—problems.

Tidal waves of worry would overtake our thinking and then flatten out into a manageable wake. My husband would be high when I was low, and then just when he slipped, I'd find the footing we needed to keep us steadied and calm. While supportive, our roller coaster of emotions didn't seem sturdy or sustainable. We were relieved when the MRI date arrived within days.

I took our son to the imaging facility, where he flirted, clicked his mouth, and giggled with the older woman next to us in the waiting room, winning her heart even though he was the one in potential peril. I explained why we were there. I tried to sound brave, but I'm not sure I fooled her.

"Morgan," a nurse called, holding the door extended. It was strange to hear my baby boy's name called, as if he had a single say in the test he was about to undergo. I felt a swell of worry, and I froze in my seat until the nice lady waiting near me leaned over.

"I think it's time for you to go back now," she said.

"Oh, right. OK," I stammered.

"You're just getting pictures today, honey. God already sees what's inside there. This will just help y'all see too. I'll be out here praying that God keeps you in perfect peace." She nodded me toward the door.

I gathered the diaper bag and my courage and followed the nurse down the hall. She took my son's vitals right away. Someone else came in with a stethoscope, and even the small-diameter side of the instrument looked enormous on his little chest. It was cold, and true to form, the sensation made him laugh.

"This little guy sure loves life, doesn't he?" the nurse asked.

"He does love life."

The statement hung in the air.

He loved life. I loved his life. A lump formed in my throat.

I thought of the Waiting Room Lady's reminder about perfect peace. I had brought my Bible to read during my son's test, and while I needed a little help from the index in the back, I found the verse she mentioned. It was Isaiah 26:3. I memorized it quickly.

The nurse administered a shot designed to put my son to sleep, but he resisted, cooed, wiggled, and—true to form—giggled. At the time we all needed him to just stop loving life for a minute and succumb to the medicine, he threatened to mess up the whole morning with happiness.

"We'll try a little more medicine, but if he doesn't fall asleep, we'll have to reschedule," the nurse said.

Within minutes he conked, a precious 15-pound sack of potatoes lying relaxed in my arms. Suddenly and irrationally, I not only insisted on placing him into the MRI tube, but also on staying in the room with him during the test. The staff advised me against it because MRIs are loud, and I had metal buckles on my belt and boots. Undeterred, I removed my belt, jewelry, watch, and shoes. They didn't say another word of protest. Someone brought a plastic chair into the room.

I inserted ear plugs and sat at an angle where I could see his tiny body at all times. Of course, my presence would make no difference in his results, but if my son moved, cried, or seemed agitated, it was going to be my touch that he felt first.

The tech gently placed miniature earphones over his tiny ears and gestured for me to place him onto the table that slid into the center of the magnet. She retreated to a sound-buffering booth.

For nearly an hour, the clicks and knocks of the MRI machine formed an incongruent soundtrack against the peace that began to wash over me. My son was just a baby. I watched him lie motionless in that little tube. But I also began to grasp that in far greater proportion to his weakness was God's strength.

• • •

Quietly, I recited the verse the Waiting Room Lady had woven into simple conversation, a promise that God would keep me in perfect peace if only I trusted Him. It gained steam in my spirit, even against the banging discord and tumble-dryer noises of the MRI machine. I must have recited the verse one hundred times.

By the end of his test, I think I'd passed my test too. My trust was set on the Lord, and I rested in the peace that no matter what the MRI revealed, my son was steadfastly in His care. It didn't make any sense. After forty-five minutes in that room, I think even the tech expected me to be hysterical and stressed.

The room quiet and well-lit now, I scooped my son's sedated little frame into my arms. He'd never looked more defenseless.

Still conked out when we arrived an hour later to our little country home, I held him in my arms, enjoying the melding of his usually busy body into mine. Not even a hard rain pelting our metal roof could detract from my sweet, settled mood. I nudged him to see if I could nurse him. Groggily, he locked eyes with mine, hungry and unaware of all that had transpired.

Less than twenty-four hours later, my cell phone rang.

The second I heard my pediatrician's voice on the line, quick tears of relief tumbled from my eyes. I knew she would never deliver bad news over the phone.

She didn't even have to tell me. I already knew. The dimple was closed—it did not extend into my son's spinal cord. My three-month-old baby could now go back to the business of being a little guy who sure loves life.

I wished I had gotten the Waiting Room Lady's name. I once again recited the gift she'd given, Isaiah 26:3, this time also calling upon God's character with gratitude-fueled relief. I did a quick diaper change and looked at the little dimple in my son's lower back, allowing myself to smile.

It was actually kind of cute.

And true to form, he smiled.

Prayer for a Peace-Filled Life

Lord, when my vulnerable, fragile state threatens my peace, help me tune out all the noise, set my mind on You, and trust You to be my peace.

Have I not commanded you? Be strong and courageous. Do not be afraid; do not be discouraged, for the LORD your God will be with you wherever you go.

Joshua 1:9 (NIV)

PEACE IN THE MOVING PIECES

By Amy Wallace

ALL IT TOOK was one email to change the course of my life.

After the furnace quit one chilly October, I emailed my landlords about the problem, never expecting this response: "We're sorry, but we can't repair the furnace, and we need to sell the house. You have to move out by January." That email came right after Thanksgiving, my last Thanksgiving in the house where I'd lived for over twenty years. The place where I'd brought two children home from the hospital. The home where I'd raised and homeschooled three amazing children.

I had nowhere to go and a job that barely paid the minimal rent I'd been paying for over two decades. I had two children on the verge of graduation, one from college and another from high school.

I panicked. Then I prayed. "Please, God, please provide a home and a job. Please let us stay here until after graduation."

• • •

We made the best of a very bleak Christmas and started packing, throwing away twenty-three years of homeschool projects and papers and giving away over half of our life.

Thankfully, the landlords relented on the January 1 move date, and we were able to stay until after my youngest graduated from high school. One prayer answered.

January 1 began my frantic search for a job. I updated my résumé and submitted many applications, prayers for a new job and a home ever-present on my lips. The ladies in the Bible study I led not only prayed but also sent me job listings, and a real estate agent looked for homes and updated us with possibilities almost daily.

Nothing happened. No callbacks. No interviews. No job meant no applying for apartments. I stopped begging God for help and started groaning without words. I tried to numb the fear with TV, drowning out the possibility that God wouldn't provide a job or a home. What would I do then?

A friend in another state far away offered a basement apartment, a small space with no kitchen, no bathtub, in a house out in the country. I'm a city girl who likes to cook and splurge on a spa day in my own bathroom. I thanked her and said no.

Months of searching, two job interviews, and a few promising possibilities of a place to live led nowhere again. I still had no job and only one unwanted home possibility.

March rolled around, the flowers in my garden started to bloom, and every day I grieved everything I would lose if I had to move into a much smaller place: pictures and books and furniture and candles and baby clothes and toys I'd saved for my children for when they started their families.

Even though it scared me to hope that God would provide, I knew somewhere deep in my heart that God had a plan and a place for us. I kept trusting the Lord, and He kept showing me in the Bible that He takes care of His children.

April came, and I had one job interview—in the place where my friend had offered me a basement apartment. The series of interviews went well, and I was sure God was opening the only door He wanted me to walk through. Then the job offer came and my start date was set. I could stop holding my breath in worry and breathe out in peace.

Movers were hired, my life was boxed up, and the truck came. Days later, we arrived in our new home and set about a whirlwind of unpacking and reorienting. I started my new job just days after we arrived.

• • •

For twenty years, I'd worked from home as a writer and a homeschool mom and then as an online teacher. Now I headed into an office filled with conversations and strangers and so much training so fast it made my head spin.

Then my apartment flooded because of plumbing problems. Seven times. Talk about the opposite of what I'd prayed for and longed for.

My new life that I'd hoped would be filled with peace and promise was instead filled with confusion and noise and floods and no solid ground. Grief overwhelmed me at every turn. I'd lost everything—my home, a life of quiet and calm that I loved, a place that made sense, friends, a church that was my home. I lost everything that made me feel like me.

So I prayed and prayed and prayed for something stable, something that felt normal, something that helped me feel like me again. Then I heard God whisper to my heart that He hadn't lost me. That I hadn't lost Him. That He was my solid ground. That reminder helped me get out of bed, but I still felt alone and unsteady in this new world of nine-to-five where nothing worked the way I was used to and nothing felt familiar. While I learned how to do the work I was given to do, it still felt overwhelming.

• • •

After a few months as an administrative assistant for a pastoral team, an office volunteer was brought in to help me on a weekly basis, an unexpected gift. One day, she asked me a question that led to a deep, tear-filled conversation.

She apologized for burdening me with her story, but I told her the entire conversation was the opposite of a burden. In the short time we'd talked and in the friendship that grew from that conversation, my grieving, numb mind and heart started to thaw. I started to feel like me again. Since I was a kid, I'd loved to listen and help people. That was why I wrote, why I taught, why I loved leading Bible study. I loved pointing people to Jesus, my Good Shepherd who calmed the waves inside and outside.

Not only did God start to calm my inside world through conversations with my new friend, but He also started to calm my outside world in a way I couldn't have imagined. Another woman joined the small group of ladies I sat with at lunch. Karen was a vibrant extrovert who instantly felt like a friend. She and I decided to start meeting once a week to journey through a counseling workbook and to talk about chaplaincy work.

I had wanted to become a chaplain a decade ago, but God had closed that door. Karen nudged the door open and nudged me through it. Within a few weeks, I'd applied, was interviewed, and received a part-time job offer to do something that felt so me I was stunned. Karen and I continued to meet and chaplain each other through many challenging situations, and I finally settled into my work, built more friendships, and found ministry opportunities at my church. I was me again even as I continued to live in that basement apartment.

Looking back, I can't say that I always trusted God or rested well during those tumultuous times, but what I do see are God's fingerprints all over every decision, every obstacle, and every unsettled moment. He carried me, quite literally, through the floods. He stilled the storm of grief from uprooting. He placed me into a new world where I have learned to depend on Him no matter how many moving pieces there are. He is my place of peace and my refuge.

Prayer for a Peace-Filled Life

Father, You are the Good Shepherd and the peace that passes all understanding. You carry us through the fires and floods of life and calm the storms. Help us run to You and find in You everything we need. Amen.

Then Jesus declared, "I am the bread of life. Whoever comes to me will never go hungry, and whoever believes in me will never be thirsty."

John 6:35 (NIV)

WE WERE CREATED incomplete with an innate desire for wholeness. If we turn to Christ to feed that hunger, we experience a joy and peace that is complete. Turning to other things that don't quench our thirst leaves us dissatisfied, causing us to reach for the wrong things. Before we know it, we become addicted to those things that will never make us replete.

In his book, *The Big Hustle*, Jim Wahlberg tells of his life growing up as the middle child of nine kids, two of whom are the famous actors Mark and Donnie. Jim had his first drink when he was eight. By the time he was eleven, he was stealing wallets to pay for cigarettes and booze. By seventeen, he was hooked on drugs and homeless. Armed robbery got him thrown into prison, where he spent most of his five-year sentence in isolation for bad behavior. It was while serving a second sentence for another armed robbery that he found God. Through a chain of events that only God could orchestrate, Jim learned firsthand that God wasn't out to punish him for his mistakes. Rather, God wanted to shower him with forgiveness and mercy, and have a relationship with him. The road to change wasn't easy for Jim, but with God by his side, he turned his life around.

He's now married with kids and committed to helping those suffering from addiction. Through his book, short films, and podcast, he wants addicts to know that "recovery is possible." But getting clean isn't enough. In his words, you'll still be left "unsatisfied and unfilled." The answer, he says, is to "bring God into the picture." True joy, he says, doesn't come from money, drugs, alcohol, or possessions but rather from a relationship with God.

Jim's story is likely not that different from our own. We may not be addicted to drugs or incarcerated for our crimes, but many of us reach for the wrong things to fill the void within. No matter what or how much we consume, whether it's food, binge-watching TV, or shopping to excess, we'll always be left unsatisfied. Christ is the only true food and drink who can satisfy our every hunger and thirst. It's by turning to Him to be filled that we are made complete.

—Claire McGarry

We can make our plans, but the Lord determines our steps.

Proverbs 16:9 (NLT)

TRUSTING HIS LEAD

By Denise Margaret Ackerman

MY HUSBAND PLACED Michelle's car seat down gently in our newly decorated nursery. I choked back silent tears and wrung shaking hands as I gazed at our beautiful, newborn 5-pound baby girl, still securely buckled inside her little seat. We had just arrived home from the hospital when myriad doubts flooded my mind. *What do I do now? Should I let her sleep or wake her up? Is she too warm in her pretty pink sweater?* My doubts and insecurity over being a new mom weighed heavy on my heart. I had little faith in my ability to raise and care for this precious gift from the Lord. I whispered a prayer, "Please help me to raise our daughter the right way."

My eight-week maternity leave swiftly vanished, and I returned to work. Exhausted from caring for our little girl, I only kept my job for two weeks before deciding to quit. Our finances suffered with the loss of my income, so I joined a direct sales business to help offset our budget. Through that venture, the Lord brought a new circle of faith-filled friends into my life.

As my friends shared their faith with me, my relationship with the Lord began to grow. The Lord also led me to a wonderful church with many strong families that gave me the support I needed to become a more confident parent. God had answered my prayer for help. He saw to it that my faith was nurtured, and I shared that spiritual growth with our budding family.

• • •

Years later, another season of testing unfolded as I struggled with different doubts and wavering faith. Michelle would soon be graduating from high school and spreading her wings to begin the next phase of her life. It was time to release her care into God's hands. But how would I ever let my precious daughter go?

My fluctuating emotions made me feel like I was participating in a tug-of-war. One moment, I would well up with pride and excitement that Michelle was going to attend college. Other times, I would lose my positive outlook as the thought of her departure filled me with dread.

We knew in our hearts that it was time to move forward, but my heart wasn't ready. Every high school activity we attended marked the brevity of our remaining time together—senior pictures, her final Christmas, and spring concerts. We shared many tearful moments as we reflected on the significant "lasts" as they slipped through our fingers. To this day, I don't know which one of us struggled more—Michelle or me. I freely admit that I was not looking forward to having my oldest leave our nest, and I have no doubts that Michelle shared the same feelings about moving away. Our mother-daughter connection grew stronger with every passing day.

As the end of her senior year approached, it was time to choose a college. Despite wavering emotions, Michelle prayerfully retreated to her cozy bedroom, brightly decorated with purple-pink walls and frilly curtains. She made a list of pros and cons as she poured through the mountain of colorful college brochures that were neatly stacked on her desk. There were many factors to consider—available courses of study, size of school, accreditation, and costs. Her hopes were set on finding a small, relatively close Christian college.

We studied her list together and narrowed it down to three schools—one in southwestern New York and two in Pennsylvania. We made plans to visit each campus, beginning with the college in New York, a three-hour drive from our remote North Country home.

We were encouraged when we arrived at the campus in record time. Feelings of awe surged inside me as we walked the welcoming grounds of the hundred-year-old university. The stately brick buildings were attractive, offset by massive maple trees showing off their bright green spring leaves. Once inside, however, the classrooms felt stiff, outdated, and uninviting. I mentioned to Michelle that the interior of the campus seemed rather beat up, but she refrained from commenting. Her demeanor was one of quiet reflection—waiting to make an assessment after visiting the next two schools.

We took a three-day weekend and traveled to her second choice: a college over five hours away. After traveling hundreds of miles, we peeled ourselves out of our small car and strolled the beautiful grounds. In some ways, the campus reminded us of the first college, except that it was larger, with an enrollment double that of the first. This school was prestigious, and our interactions with our student guide gave us the sense that it was important to "measure up" in order to attend. Once again, Michelle privately weighed the pros and cons of the visit. Weary from our long day of travel, we retired for the night at a nearby hotel. I continued to struggle with the reality that our daughter was old enough to leave us. As I tossed and turned, I wondered if every mother found this process so difficult.

The next morning, we drove across the state of Pennsylvania to check out college number three. This large campus felt sterile and lacked the charm of the previous two. I had a hard time imagining our country girl settling into the state-of-the-art atmosphere. Our time there was limited, and we packed ourselves back in the car and headed north. The long drive home gave us plenty of time to consider this important decision.

• • •

It was midnight by the time we got home. With exhausted bodies and heavy hearts, we dragged our suitcases into the house. My husband and I desired God's best placement for our daughter, but our plans did not yield the outcome we had anticipated—each visit left us feeling discouraged. None of the colleges gave us an indication that they were the right choice, and there were no other colleges that Michelle was interested in.

As we began unpacking our traveling snacks, Michelle and I spotted the Cedarville University postcard sitting atop the stack of mail on the counter. The instant our eyes met, we knew we needed to visit the college located two states away. The university's excellent reputation was well known. Our friend's daughter was a Cedarville graduate, and she had nothing but positive reviews about her experience.

After a 600-mile journey, we arrived in southwestern Ohio on Cedarville's open-house weekend. There were activities, tours, and special speakers that addressed the visiting students and their families. We convinced Michelle to spend the night on campus, staying in the girls' dorm with other potential students. As her dad and I drove to a nearby hotel, a sense of calm settled over my heart. Our daughter would soon be on her own. Instead of dread, that thought now brought a sense of peace.

Once we returned home, the final decision rested in Michelle's hands. We prayed for the next several days while she deliberated. As she mulled over the four schools, Cedarville repeatedly rose to the top of her list. Even though it was much farther away than she felt comfortable with, it was the only college that felt right. Decision made. Application sent. Then, the wait.

An envelope with crisp blue lettering spelling out "Cedarville" stood out from all the other pieces of correspondence in our mailbox that day. Michelle and I held our breath as she cradled the envelope containing life-changing information in her hands. I studied her face for a reaction as she tentatively unfolded the letter. Her hazel eyes brightened, and a relieved smile spread across her sweet face as she proudly announced, "Accepted!"

That evening, as Michelle headed to bed, a weight of uncertainty hung in the air. We hugged goodnight, and a few minutes later she came back down the stairs holding an inspirational plaque in her hands.

"Mom, I don't think God wants us to worry about this decision to go to Cedarville." She held out the plaque. "This fell off the shelf and into my hands after I finished brushing my teeth."

God whispered words of reassurance to each of our hearts as we recited together the faith-filled words displayed on the little plaque: "The will of God will never lead you where the grace of God cannot keep you." The Lord provided encouragement in an unusual way that evening, and we both decided that we would choose to trust His grace for this journey.

Prayer for a Peace-Filled Life

Dear Heavenly Father, thank You for guiding us and giving us peace as we step out in faith to follow You. As I pray and study Your Word, please help me to trust You in every area of my life and with the lives of those I love.

BIBLICAL PROMISES OF PEACE

All scriptures from NIV translation.

Acts 9:31	Then the church throughout Judea, Galilee and Samaria enjoyed a time of peace and was strengthened. Living in the fear of the Lord and encouraged by the Holy Spirit, it increased in numbers.
Colossians 3:2	Set your minds on things above, not on earthly things.
Colossians 3:13	Bear with each other and forgive one another if any of you has a grievance against someone. Forgive as the Lord forgave you.
Colossians 3:15	Let the peace of Christ rule in your hearts, since as members of one body you were called to peace. And be thankful.
1 Corinthians 14:33	For God is not a God of disorder but of peace—as in all the congregations of the Lord's people.
2 Corinthians 5:7	For we live by faith, not by sight.
2 Corinthians 8:12	For if the willingness is there, the gift is acceptable according to what one has, not according to what one does not have.
2 Corinthians 13:11	Finally, brothers and sisters, rejoice! Strive for full restoration, encourage one another, be of one mind, live in peace. And the God of love and peace will be with you.
Daniel 10:19	"Do not be afraid, you who are highly esteemed," he said. "Peace! Be strong now; be strong." When he spoke to me, I was strengthened and said, "Speak, my lord, since you have given me strength."
Deuteronomy 31:6	Be strong and courageous. Do not be afraid or terrified because of them, for the LORD your God goes with you; he will never leave you nor forsake you.

Deuteronomy 31:8	The Lord himself goes before you and will be with you; he will never leave you nor forsake you. Do not be afraid; do not be discouraged.
Ecclesiastes 5:18–20	This is what I have observed to be good: that it is appropriate for a person to eat, to drink and to find satisfaction in their toilsome labor under the sun during the few days of life God has given them—for this is their lot. Moreover, when God gives someone wealth and possessions, and the ability to enjoy them, to accept their lot and be happy in their toil—this is a gift of God. They seldom reflect on the days of their life, because God keeps them occupied with gladness of heart.
Ephesians 2:14	For he himself is our peace, who has made the two groups one and has destroyed the barrier, the dividing wall of hostility.
Ephesians 4:2–4	Be completely humble and gentle; be patient, bearing with one another in love. Make every effort to keep the unity of the Spirit through the bond of peace. There is one body and one Spirit, just as you were called to one hope when you were called.
Ephesians 6:1–4	Children, obey your parents in the Lord, for this is right. "Honor your father and mother"—which is the first commandment with a promise—"so that it may go well with you and that you may enjoy long life on the earth." Fathers, do not exasperate your children; instead, bring them up in the training and instruction of the Lord.
Ephesians 6:14–15	Stand firm then, with the belt of truth buckled around your waist, with the breastplate of righteousness in place, and with your feet fitted with the readiness that comes from the gospel of peace.
Exodus 33:14	The Lord replied, "My Presence will go with you, and I will give you rest."
Galatians 5:22–23	But the fruit of the Spirit is love, joy, peace, forbearance, kindness, goodness, faithfulness, gentleness and self-control. Against such things there is no law.

Hebrews 4:11	Let us, therefore, make every effort to enter that rest, so that no one will perish by following their example of disobedience.
Hebrews 12:11	No discipline seems pleasant at the time, but painful. Later on, however, it produces a harvest of righteousness and peace for those who have been trained by it.
Hebrews 12:14	Make every effort to live in peace with everyone and to be holy; without holiness no one will see the Lord.
Hebrews 13:2	Do not forget to show hospitality to strangers, for by so doing some people have shown hospitality to angels without knowing it.
Hebrews 13:5	Keep your lives free from the love of money and be content with what you have, because God has said, "Never will I leave you; never will I forsake you."
Hebrews 13:20–21	Now may the God of peace, who through the blood of the eternal covenant brought back from the dead our Lord Jesus, that great Shepherd of the sheep, equip you with everything good for doing his will, and may he work in us what is pleasing to him, through Jesus Christ, to whom be glory for ever and ever. Amen.
Isaiah 2:4	He will judge between the nations and will settle disputes for many peoples. They will beat their swords into plowshares and their spears into pruning hooks. Nation will not take up sword against nation, nor will they train for war anymore.
Isaiah 9:6	For to us a child is born, to us a son is given, and the government will be on his shoulders. And he will be called Wonderful Counselor, Mighty God, Everlasting Father, Prince of Peace.
Isaiah 12:2	Surely God is my salvation; I will trust and not be afraid. The LORD, the LORD himself, is my strength and my defense; he has become my salvation.
Isaiah 26:3	You will keep in perfect peace those whose minds are steadfast, because they trust in you.

Isaiah 26:12	Lord, you establish peace for us; all that we have accomplished you have done for us.
Isaiah 30:21	Whether you turn to the right or to the left, your ears will hear a voice behind you, saying, "This is the way; walk in it."
Isaiah 32:17–18	The fruit of that righteousness will be peace; its effect will be quietness and confidence forever. My people will live in peaceful dwelling places, in secure homes, in undisturbed places of rest.
Isaiah 41:10	So do not fear, for I am with you; do not be dismayed, for I am your God. I will strengthen you and help you; I will uphold you with my righteous right hand.
Isaiah 48:22	"There is no peace," says the Lord, "for the wicked."
Isaiah 52:7	How beautiful on the mountains are the feet of those who bring good news, who proclaim peace, who bring good tidings, who proclaim salvation, who say to Zion, "Your God reigns!"
Isaiah 53:5	But he was pierced for our transgressions, he was crushed for our iniquities; the punishment that brought us peace was on him, and by his wounds we are healed.
Isaiah 54:10	"Though the mountains be shaken and the hills be removed, yet my unfailing love for you will not be shaken nor my covenant of peace be removed," says the Lord, who has compassion on you.
Isaiah 54:13	All your children will be taught by the Lord, and great will be their peace.
Isaiah 55:12	You will go out in joy and be led forth in peace; the mountains and hills will burst into song before you, and all the trees of the field will clap their hands.
Isaiah 66:12	For this is what the Lord says: "I will extend peace to her like a river, and the wealth of nations like a flooding stream; you will nurse and be carried on her arm and dandled on her knees."

James 1:2–4	Consider it pure joy, my brothers and sisters, whenever you face trials of many kinds, because you know that the testing of your faith produces perseverance. Let perseverance finish its work so that you may be mature and complete, not lacking anything.
James 1:12	Blessed is the one who perseveres under trial because, having stood the test, that person will receive the crown of life that the Lord has promised to those who love him.
James 2:14	What good is it, my brothers and sisters, if someone claims to have faith but has no deeds? Can such faith save them?
James 3:17–18	But the wisdom that comes from heaven is first of all pure; then peace-loving, considerate, submissive, full of mercy and good fruit, impartial and sincere. Peacemakers who sow in peace reap a harvest of righteousness.
Jeremiah 29:11	"For I know the plans I have for you," declares the LORD, "plans to prosper you and not to harm you, plans to give you hope and a future."
Jeremiah 31:25	I will refresh the weary and satisfy the faint.
Jeremiah 33:6	Nevertheless, I will bring health and healing to it; I will heal my people and will let them enjoy abundant peace and security.
Job 22:21–22	Submit to God and be at peace with him; in this way prosperity will come to you. Accept instruction from his mouth and lay up his words in your heart.
John 3:16–17	For God so loved the world that he gave his one and only Son, that whoever believes in him shall not perish but have eternal life. For God did not send his Son into the world to condemn the world, but to save the world through him.
John 14:27	Peace I leave with you; my peace I give you. I do not give to you as the world gives. Do not let your hearts be troubled and do not be afraid.

John 16:33	I have told you these things, so that in me you may have peace. In this world you will have trouble. But take heart! I have overcome the world.
John 20:21	Again Jesus said, "Peace be with you! As the Father has sent me, I am sending you.
1 John 1:9	If we confess our sins, he is faithful and just and will forgive us our sins and purify us from all unrighteousness.
2 John 1:3	Grace, mercy and peace from God the Father and from Jesus Christ, the Father's Son, will be with us in truth and love.
2 John 6	As you have heard from the beginning, his command is that you walk in love.
Jude 1:1–2	To those who have been called, who are loved in God the Father and kept for Jesus Christ: Mercy, peace and love be yours in abundance.
Judges 18:6	The priest answered them, "Go in peace. Your journey has the LORD's approval."
Leviticus 26:6	I will grant peace in the land, and you will lie down and no one will make you afraid. I will remove wild beasts from the land, and the sword will not pass through your country.
Luke 1:76–79	And you, my child, will be called a prophet of the Most High; for you will go on before the Lord to prepare the way for him, to give his people the knowledge of salvation through the forgiveness of their sins, because of the tender mercy of our God, by which the rising sun will come to us from heaven to shine on those living in darkness and in the shadow of death, to guide our feet into the path of peace.
Luke 2:13–14	Suddenly a great company of the heavenly host appeared with the angel, praising God and saying, "Glory to God in the highest heaven, and on earth peace to those on whom his favor rests."

Luke 10:5	When you enter a house, first say, "Peace to this house."
Luke 24:36	While they were still talking about this, Jesus himself stood among them and said to them, "Peace be with you."
Malachi 2:5	My covenant was with him, a covenant of life and peace, and I gave them to him; this called for reverence and he revered me and stood in awe of my name.
Mark 4:39	He got up, rebuked the wind and said to the waves, "Quiet! Be still!" Then the wind died down and it was completely calm.
Mark 9:50	"Salt is good, but if it loses its saltiness, how can you make it salty again? Have salt among yourselves, and be at peace with each other.
Matthew 5:9	Blessed are the peacemakers, for they will be called children of God.
Matthew 6:34	Therefore do not worry about tomorrow, for tomorrow will worry about itself. Each day has enough trouble of its own.
Matthew 11:28–30	Come to me, all you who are weary and burdened, and I will give you rest. Take my yoke upon you and learn from me, for I am gentle and humble in heart, and you will find rest for your souls. For my yoke is easy and my burden is light.
Numbers 6:24–26	The LORD bless you and keep you; the LORD make his face shine on you and be gracious to you; the LORD turn his face toward you and give you peace.
1 Peter 3:9	Do not repay evil with evil or insult with insult. On the contrary, repay evil with blessing, because to this you were called so that you may inherit a blessing.
1 Peter 3:11	They must turn from evil and do good; they must seek peace and pursue it.

1 Peter 5:6–7	Humble yourselves, therefore, under God's mighty hand, that he may lift you up in due time. Cast all your anxiety on him because he cares for you.
2 Peter 1:2	Grace and peace be yours in abundance through the knowledge of God and of Jesus our Lord.
2 Peter 1:10–11	Therefore, my brothers and sisters, make every effort to confirm your calling and election. For if you do these things, you will never stumble, and you will receive a rich welcome into the eternal kingdom of our Lord and Savior Jesus Christ.
2 Peter 3:14	So then, dear friends, since you are looking forward to this, make every effort to be found spotless, blameless and at peace with him.
Philemon 3	Grace and peace to you from God our Father and the Lord Jesus Christ.
Philippians 4:6–7	Do not be anxious about anything, but in every situation, by prayer and petition, with thanksgiving, present your requests to God. And the peace of God, which transcends all understanding, will guard your hearts and your minds in Christ Jesus.
Philippians 4:9	Whatever you have learned or received or heard from me, or seen in me—put it into practice. And the God of peace will be with you.
Philippians 4:12–13	I have learned the secret of being content in any and every situation, whether well fed or hungry, whether living in plenty or in want. I can do all this through him who gives me strength.
Proverbs 1:33	But whoever listens to me will live in safety and be at ease, without fear of harm.
Proverbs 3:1–2	My son, do not forget my teaching, but keep my commands in your heart, for they will prolong your life many years and bring you peace and prosperity.

Proverbs 3:16–18	Long life is in her right hand; in her left hand are riches and honor. Her ways are pleasant ways, and all her paths are peace. She is a tree of life to those who take hold of her; those who hold her fast will be blessed.
Proverbs 3:24	When you lie down, you will not be afraid; when you lie down, your sleep will be sweet.
Proverbs 12:20	Deceit is in the hearts of those who plot evil, but those who promote peace have joy.
Proverbs 16:7	When the LORD takes pleasure in anyone's way, he causes their enemies to make peace with them.
Proverbs 16:32	Better a patient person than a warrior, one with self-control than one who takes a city.
Proverbs 17:1	Better a dry crust with peace and quiet than a house full of feasting, with strife.
Psalm 4:8	In peace I will lie down and sleep, for you alone, LORD, make me dwell in safety.
Psalm 9:9–10	The Lord is a refuge for the oppressed, a stronghold in times of trouble. Those who know your name trust in you, for you, Lord, have never forsaken those who seek you.
Psalm 19:1	The heavens declare the glory of God; the skies proclaim the work of his hands.
Psalm 23:1–3	The LORD is my shepherd, I lack nothing. He makes me lie down in green pastures, he leads me beside quiet waters, he refreshes my soul. He guides me along the right paths for his name's sake.
Psalm 25:4	Show me your ways, LORD, teach me your paths.
Psalm 27:14	Wait for the LORD; be strong and take heart and wait for the LORD.
Psalm 29:11	The LORD gives strength to his people; the LORD blesses his people with peace.

Psalm 32:7	You are my hiding place; you will protect me from trouble and surround me with songs of deliverance.
Psalm 34:12–13	Whoever of you loves life and desires to see many good days, keep your tongue from evil and your lips from telling lies.
Psalm 34:14–15	Turn from evil and do good; seek peace and pursue it. The eyes of the LORD are on the righteous, and his ears are attentive to their cry.
Psalm 37:7	Be still before the LORD and wait patiently for him.
Psalm 37:11	But the meek will inherit the land and enjoy peace and prosperity.
Psalm 37:37	Consider the blameless, observe the upright; a future awaits those who seek peace.
Psalm 46:1–3	God is our refuge and strength, an ever-present help in trouble. Therefore we will not fear, though the earth give way and the mountains fall into the heart of the sea, though its waters roar and foam and the mountains quake with their surging.
Psalm 46:10	He says, "Be still, and know that I am God; I will be exalted among the nations, I will be exalted in the earth."
Psalm 55:18	He rescues me unharmed from the battle waged against me, even though many oppose me.
Psalm 62:1	Truly my soul finds rest in God; my salvation comes from him.
Psalm 72:7	In his days may the righteous flourish and prosperity abound till the moon is no more.
Psalm 85:8	I will listen to what God the LORD says; he promises peace to his people, his faithful servants—but let them not turn to folly.
Psalm 85:10	Love and faithfulness meet together; righteousness and peace kiss each other.

Psalm 119:165	Great peace have those who love your law, and nothing can make them stumble.
Psalm 122:6–7	Pray for the peace of Jerusalem: "May those who love you be secure. May there be peace within your walls and security within your citadels."
Romans 1:7	To all in Rome who are loved by God and called to be his holy people: Grace and peace to you from God our Father and from the Lord Jesus Christ.
Romans 2:7–8	To those who by persistence in doing good seek glory, honor and immortality, he will give eternal life. But for those who are self-seeking and who reject the truth and follow evil, there will be wrath and anger.
Romans 5:1–2	Therefore, since we have been justified through faith, we have peace with God through our Lord Jesus Christ, through whom we have gained access by faith into this grace in which we now stand. And we boast in the hope of the glory of God.
Romans 6:23	For the wages of sin is death, but the gift of God is eternal life in Christ Jesus our Lord.
Romans 8:6	The mind governed by the flesh is death, but the mind governed by the Spirit is life and peace.
Romans 12:2	Do not conform to the pattern of this world, but be transformed by the renewing of your mind. Then you will be able to test and approve what God's will is—his good, pleasing and perfect will.
Romans 12:17	Do not repay anyone evil for evil. Be careful to do what is right in the eyes of everyone.
Romans 12:18	If it is possible, as far as it depends on you, live at peace with everyone.
Romans 14:17–19	For the kingdom of God is not a matter of eating and drinking, but of righteousness, peace and joy in the Holy Spirit, because anyone who serves Christ in this way is pleasing to God and receives human approval. Let us therefore make every effort to do what leads to peace and to mutual edification.

Romans 15:13	May the God of hope fill you with all joy and peace as you trust in him, so that you may overflow with hope by the power of the Holy Spirit.
Romans 15:33	The God of peace be with you all. Amen.
Romans 16:20	The God of peace will soon crush Satan under your feet. The grace of our Lord Jesus be with you.
1 Thessalonians 5:3	While people are saying, "Peace and safety," destruction will come on them suddenly, as labor pains on a pregnant woman, and they will not escape.
1 Thessalonians 5:15	Make sure that nobody pays back wrong for wrong, but always strive to do what is good for each other and for everyone else.
1 Thessalonians 5:23	May God himself, the God of peace, sanctify you through and through. May your whole spirit, soul and body be kept blameless at the coming of our Lord Jesus Christ.
2 Thessalonians 3:16	Now may the Lord of peace himself give you peace at all times and in every way. The Lord be with all of you.
1 Timothy 2:1–2	I urge, then, first of all, that petitions, prayers, intercession and thanksgiving be made for all people—for kings and all those in authority, that we may live peaceful and quiet lives in all godliness and holiness.
1 Timothy 6:6-7	But godliness with contentment is great gain. For we brought nothing into the world, and we can take nothing out of it.
2 Timothy 1:7	For the Spirit God gave us does not make us timid, but gives us power, love and self-discipline.
2 Timothy 2:22	Flee the evil desires of youth and pursue righteousness, faith, love and peace, along with those who call on the Lord out of a pure heart.

Titus 1:8–9	Rather, he must be hospitable, one who loves what is good, who is self-controlled, upright, holy and disciplined. He must hold firmly to the trustworthy message as it has been taught, so that he can encourage others by sound doctrine and refute those who oppose it.
Zechariah 8:16	These are the things you are to do: Speak the truth to each other, and render true and sound judgment in your courts.
Zechariah 8:19	Therefore love truth and peace.
Zechariah 9:10	I will take away the chariots from Ephraim and the warhorses from Jerusalem, and the battle bow will be broken. He will proclaim peace to the nations. His rule will extend from sea to sea and from the River to the ends of the earth.
Zephaniah 3:17	The LORD your God is with you, the Mighty Warrior who saves. He will take great delight in you; in his love he will no longer rebuke you, but will rejoice over you with singing.

A NOTE FROM THE EDITORS

We hope you enjoyed *Exploring God's Promises: Peace,* published by Guideposts. For over seventy-five years, Guideposts, a nonprofit organization, has been driven by a vision of a world filled with hope. We aspire to be the voice of a trusted friend, a friend who makes you feel more hopeful and connected.

By making a purchase from Guideposts, you join our community in touching millions of lives, inspiring them to believe that all things are possible through faith, hope, and prayer. Your continued support allows us to provide uplifting resources to those in need. Whether through our communities, websites, apps, or publications, we inspire our audiences, bring them together, and comfort, uplift, entertain, and guide them. Visit us at guideposts.org to learn more.

We would love to hear from you. Write us at Guideposts, P.O. Box 5815, Harlan, Iowa 51593 or call us at (800) 932-2145. Did you love *Exploring God's Promises: Peace*? Leave a review for this product on guideposts.org/shop. Your feedback helps others in our community find relevant products.

Printed in the United States
by Baker & Taylor Publisher Services